That They Might Seek Him

That They Might Seek Him

Introduction to Migration Ministry

Steven B. Kern

Foreword by Anthony F. Casey

WIPF & STOCK · Eugene, Oregon

THAT THEY MIGHT SEEK HIM
Introduction to Migration Ministry

Copyright © 2021 Steven B. Kern. All rights reserved. Except for brief quotations in critical publications or reviews, no part of this book may be reproduced in any manner without prior written permission from the publisher. Write: Permissions, Wipf and Stock Publishers, 199 W. 8th Ave., Suite 3, Eugene, OR 97401.

Wipf & Stock
An Imprint of Wipf and Stock Publishers
199 W. 8th Ave., Suite 3
Eugene, OR 97401

www.wipfandstock.com

PAPERBACK ISBN: 978-1-7252-8424-1
HARDCOVER ISBN: 978-1-7252-8425-8
EBOOK ISBN: 978-1-7252-8426-5

05/07/21

Scripture quotations taken from the (NASB®) New American Standard Bible®, copyright © 1960, 1971, 1977, 1995, 2020 by The Lockman Foundation. Used by permission. All rights reserved. www.lockman.org.

Table 6.1, "Indicators of Integration Framework," reproduced from *Home Office Indicators of Integration framework 2019, Third Edition*. Used by permission.

To Jesus Christ, who "purchased people for God with [his] blood from every tribe, language, people, and nation" (Rev 5:9). You have given my life purpose!

And He made from one man every nation of mankind to live on all the face of the earth, having determined their appointed times and the boundaries of their habitation, *that they would seek God*, if perhaps they might feel around for Him and find Him, though He is not far from each one of us.

—ACTS 17:26–27 (EMPHASIS ADDED)

Contents

Tables and Figures | ix
Foreword by Anthony F. Casey | xi
Preface | xiii
Acknowledgements | xv
Introduction | xvii

1. Sharpening Contemporary Focus on a Timeless Phenomenon | 1
2. Developing a Theology of Migration | 21
3. Defining Ministry to Migrants | 39
4. Understanding the Political Context | 55
5. Responding to Immigration Policy Development | 74
6. Taking Steps Toward Contextualization and Integration | 94
7. Engaging Migrants in a Digital World | 113
8. Planning Your Strategy | 130

Bibliography | 147

Tables and Figures

Table 1.1. Migration According to Continent in 2017 | 8
Table 1.2. Top Ten Immigrant Host Countries in 2017 | 9
Table 1.3. Top Ten Immigrant Source Countries in 2017 | 9–10
Figure 4.1. Paradigms of International Relations | 59
Table 6.1. Indicators of Integration Framework | 103

Foreword

Migration and mission are perhaps the most pressing topics in front of the global church in recent decades. Globalization coupled with the push and pull factors of economic development, changing political policy, wars, and climate displacement has led to peoples on the move at a pace rivalling any experienced throughout history. Many have written that the nations are at our doorstep here in the United States, but in reality, global migration means people from everywhere are going everywhere.

Often, churches find themselves surrounded by changing communities, resettled refugees, apartments filled with international students, and ethnic businesses springing up every month. Many churches find themselves at a loss as to how to respond, and often do not respond at all. Other times, churches react in a kneejerk fashion without any real strategy for engaging these new migrants in their communities. Mission to migrants occurs on the periphery as the church carries on with ministry as usual.

In the face of this reality Steve Kern has written a timely and valuable book to not only aid the church in reaching migrants, but to begin to help reshape their entire paradigm of God's redemptive plan. Kern challenges his readers to not just react to the global migration movement, but to participate in something God has been doing since the beginning of Scripture—calling to himself a people from every tribe, tongue, and nation.

Kern's goal is to provide a well-researched book on the contours of global migration, God's passionate commitment to loving the sojourner, and a practical guide for the local church to respond, embrace, and join in God's redemptive plan. To this end, Kern brings clarity and precision to what can sometimes be muddy waters. This book presents the complex nuances of global migration patterns and migrants themselves. Kern shows that migration is not out of God's control, but on the contrary, is and always has been at the core of God's plan of redemption throughout the storyline of Scripture. Kern addresses the political drivers of global migration along with an analysis of immigration policy from around the world. Finally, he offers a wealth of practical strategies the church may use in their own contextual situations.

Especially helpful in this work is Kern's engagement with difficult issues in a non-reductionistic fashion. Kern explores issues related to mono- or multiethnic church in migrant ministry, how migrant ministry has revitalized dying churches, and how the church might view local, national, and international political policy related to migration in a fresh, biblical way.

That They Might Seek Him is a wonderful blend of scholarship coupled with inspiring and convicting stories and practical examples that leave the reader motivated and equipped to take action. The book is well suited for use in university and seminary classes on migration ministry as well as by local churches looking for guidance as they encounter one of the greatest opportunities of our lifetime. Peoples are on the move; God is on the move. The question is, will the church join?

Anthony Casey, PhD
Associate Professor of Intercultural Studies
William Carey University

Preface

IN MANY WAYS, THE thoughts for this book were birthed at a time when migration related issues were front and center for much of the world. It was 2015, the atrocities leading to the Syrian refugee crisis were like permanent fixtures in the news cycles. Videos, pictures, and stories of men, women, and children in pursuit of safety and a better life moved individuals and nations to action. Ironically and concurrently, immigration issues were passionately debated in anticipation of the U.S. presidential election. Candidates and citizens chose positions on policies and structures that would best serve their nation as they dealt with the difficult topic of irregular immigration.

Beyond the plight of asylum seekers and the politics of immigrant status, God was at work. He was orchestrating the times and places of people from the nations. He was doing that intentionally, "that they might seek him" (Acts 17:26–28).

It was not as if God first began to do that in 2015. But that is when he grabbed my heart with that truth. It is to the reality of his purpose in migration, then, that I committed a large portion of my PhD focus. And it is to that reality that I envision committing a large portion of the next phase of my life. It is also with that reality in mind that I have written these lines.

This book represents what I wish I had in 2015: an introduction to migrant ministry. I have intentionally included the word "introduction" in the full title. In these lines, I have intentionally avoided an assumption that the reader has vast previous knowledge. After all, that is where I began. Similarly, I have restrained from diving so deep that the reader is quickly in over his or her head.

That They Might Seek Him has both the academician and the practitioner in mind. It incorporates some of the best research and practical insights from others who have studied and worked extensively in this field. In that regard, the content here is not unique. True, many of these ideas can be found elsewhere. Still, the book is purposefully compiled with those in mind who are embarking on a journey of study and ministry among migrants.

Consequently, the book explores contemporary migration realities through the lens of the timeless Scriptures with a view to practical application. Care is taken to address the nature and priorities of migration ministry. Given the present challenges of policy development, academic background and biblical principles are offered to help believers navigate these waters. Since ministry contextualization and migrant integration offer unique challenges for believers engaging in migrant ministry, these issues comprise an entire chapter. Even though migration came to a virtual standstill during the global pandemic of COVID-19, migrant ministry did not. The approach did have to change. Thus, this book identifies some of the innovative ways in which digital tools can be utilized for the temporal welfare and eternal blessing of those who have migrated.

In short, it is my hope that this book serves to equip you, the reader, to develop a strategy to more passionately and fruitfully understand and engage in migrant ministry.

Acknowledgements

THE LINES THAT FOLLOW represent much sacrifice. But the sacrifice to which I wish to draw attention is not my own. It is that of countless Christian workers who have given of themselves in order to touch the lives of migrants. I have observed, interviewed, emailed, and truly been inspired by dozens of you. Your sacrifice to meet both temporal and eternal needs in the name of Jesus will reap eternal rewards.

In addition, I could list many, whose lives have blessed mine by providing important input during this process. Unfortunately, space only permits me to point to a few.

Thank you, Esther Katz. Your life and ministry encouraged me to open my eyes to the nations that were in Germany in the 1990s. You may never even be aware of this book, but you were a big part of it!

Albrecht Seibold's kingdom minded generosity in sharing time and contacts with me was more than I ever could have expected.

Dr. Anthony Casey's expertise in the field and love for the writing process, offered great insight and helpful directives.

Celeste Kern's joyful and sacrificial commitment to me, to others, and to Jesus provided me with constant inspiration to keep writing.

Introduction

Throughout the last twenty years, the pendulum swings of responses towards migration have been, at times, sudden and extreme. In September of 2001, immigrants were reportedly the cause of terrorist attacks on New York City and Washington, D.C. The pendulum swung overnight as politicians began to rethink immigration policy and vetting practices. At the same time, many around the world looked with sudden suspicion at those who were guests in their country—many of whom they had overlooked the day before.

Ten years later, the pendulum swung once again. As civil war broke out in Syria in 2011, millions fled to other countries. The world watched news reports and social media posts, and their hearts grieved for their fellow man. Nations opened their doors to refugees and asylum seekers. Residents welcomed them with signs and an outpouring of hospitable generosity.

But, by 2015, many countries began to feel the full weight of having welcomed so many. Their new guests were not acclimating to their new homes as quickly as many hoped. The price paid in terms of economic impact seemed high. Simultaneously, irregular immigration became a topic of concern for both the European Union and the United States. Thus, the pendulum swung back in the opposite direction.

Still, the most powerful pendulum swing of policy, practices, and emotion with regard to the migration of people came in 2020. As a result of the global COVID-19 pandemic, migration and international travel came to a virtual standstill. Anyone entering a country not their own had to have an exceptional reason to travel and/or be willing to be tested or to quarantine for two weeks.

The purpose of this book is not ultimately to provide a detailed account of events that have led to an ever-changing public opinion of migrants and immigration. But, let's face it, your own perspective has likely

Introduction

been formed or at least impacted by these recent historical realities. If you aren't careful, immigration can become a problem to resolve, and the migrants themselves can blur into nameless, faceless pawns in a game where the rules must be changed so that nations "win."

Even though the lines that follow will, at times, address some of the historical and present-day political realities of migration, their goal is to identify God's purposes in migration. It is true that there are many migration problems to solve. For the believer, however, migration represents an opportunity to engage. After all, migrants are individuals with a past and a future—an eternal one at that.

This book, then, will *inform* you, the reader, about widespread migration realities. It will *inspire* you with divine perspective about the migrant living in your neighborhood or in another nation. It will *equip* you with practical tools and resources to use among those who are not only on the move but also, whether they know it or not, on the search for God.

1

Sharpening Contemporary Focus on a Timeless Phenomenon

In the late twentieth century, the social climate in Germany was volatile. German citizens were learning how to live together after the fall of the Wall and the reunification of the former East and West. In addition, one did not have to dig too deep to discover the realities of Ausländerhass (hatred of foreigners) among some. In its extreme forms, this hatred was directed largely at Turkish guest workers and other internationals seeking asylum. Neo-Nazi skinheads not only participated in aggressive demonstrations, but they also carried out arson attacks on buildings housing asylum seekers. These attacks killed or injured many migrants.

To be sure, most German citizens were opposed to these extreme acts of aggression. Still, the majority of them were not exactly extending a hearty welcome to their international neighbors. Many were not much more than tolerant of the presence of these foreigners on German soil. Even Christ followers made minimal attempts to demonstrate compassion towards these others created in the image of God. Instead, they often responded to the presence of these refugees with eye rolls, jokes, and passivity.[1]

Esther, on the other hand, was an exception. She was a godly German woman living in the northeastern Black Forest area. She had a huge heart for welcoming these migrants and reaching them for Christ. She engaged in a holistic ministry of meeting material needs while addressing their

1. The author was present in Germany at that time and, at times, just as negligent.

ultimate need of a relationship with Jesus. My wife and I served as missionaries in Germany at the time. Esther was part of our fledgling church. She invited us to participate in this ministry among migrants. My response was a token one. I agreed to lead a monthly Bible study/discussion. And that is exactly what I did—nothing more, nothing less. After all, I had gone to Germany to reach Germans, not these immigrant wanderers (although I was one myself). Consequently, I limited my involvement to those couple of hours a month.

Looking back now, I wish that I had more fully grasped the incredible gospel opportunity at my front door. If only I had recognized that my choice did not have to be either Germans or migrants. It could have been both. If only I would have understood the unique kairos moment (Eph 5:15–16) afforded me and invested more time and focus on reaching these people on the move.

And that is my prayer for you.

BIBLE BELIEVERS TRACE HUMAN origins from a couple named Adam and Eve and from a place called Eden. There is no mistaking the fact that men and women have, from the dawn of their existence, multiplied and, from the place of their origin, migrated. They have responded, sometimes voluntarily, sometimes out of necessity, to God's mandate to "be fruitful and increase in number; fill the earth" (Gen 1:28). Migration, then, is nothing new.

Divine promptings and economic, political, relational, geographic, and climate realities influence the locations where people stay as well as the destinations of their migration. Abraham responded to an invitation to go to a land promised him. Israelites later sought freedom from Egyptian bondage and returned to this land. The people of Israel and of Judah were taken into exile in Assyria and Babylon respectively. Jesus and his parents fled for safety to Egypt.

Fast-forward to today. Chinese students move to the United States, where they pursue a cross-cultural education. Sri Lankan women migrate to Dubai to offer care services and benefit from the economic boom. Syrians flee to Germany in pursuit of safety and in hopes of a fresh start. Motivated by all kinds of influences, millions throughout the millennia of time have

Sharpening Contemporary Focus on a Timeless Phenomenon

moved and millions in the present day continue to move from the place of their origin or citizenship to other locations outside of their homeland.

Migration is, indeed, nothing new. Its historical roots make it clear that it is an ancient phenomenon as old as humankind itself. At the same time, its contemporary expressions give no indications that it will soon stop. Experts indicate that there were an estimated 258 million migrants in 2017. In other words, some 3.4 percent of the world population are migrants.[2] To put that number in perspective, if those migrants were numbered as part of the same country, theirs would be the fifth largest nation in the world.[3]

Not only is migration not a new experience; it is also not a recent revival of an ancient, but until-recently-dormant phenomenon. One can read about it in the movement of God's people into Egypt or their return more than four hundred years later. Between the seventeenth and nineteenth centuries, European and Asian migration was instrumental in the populating of North America. The flow of people from one land to another has been a consistent part of human existence and it has been relatively constant over the last decades. In fact, while the total number of migrants has grown over the last sixty years, the percentage of the total global population on the move has remained relatively stable at roughly 3 percent.[4]

As a result of this ancient, more recent, and contemporary migration, people inhabit the seven continents of the world today. To be sure, the distribution is not even. A dry country like Namibia has a sparse population density of roughly three people per square kilometer.[5] In contrast, Bangladesh has a density of more than 1,100 people per square kilometer.[6] But the Philippines boasts the most densely populated city in the world as Manila has more than 46,100 people per square kilometer.[7]

Although they are dispersed unevenly, people are now spread to the proverbial "four corners" of the globe. This book explores some of God's purposes in the movement of people depicted in Scripture. It traces some of the more recent reasons for migration. Policies that govern their immigration into new lands will also be explored. But all of these topics are

---

2. Vidal and Tjaden, *Global Migration Indicators 2018*, 18.
3. US Census Bureau, "Current Population."
4. Haas et al., *Age of Migration*, 4.
5. World Population Review, "Namibia Population 2020."
6. World Population Review, "Bangladesh Population 2020."
7. S. Wright, "World's Most Densely Populated Cities."

considered here for the purpose of better understanding how to reach and disciple those on the move.

Understanding Today's Terms

Before meeting the world's modern migrants, it is important to grasp some basic terms that will be used in this chapter and throughout the book. The list of migration vocabulary terms that follows is certainly not exhaustive. Other essential words will be introduced where needed and as needed. Nevertheless, these outline some key words that merit noting from the outset.

A *migrant* is a "person who moves away from his or her place of usual residence, whether within a country or across an international border."[8] In order to bring uniformity to the statistical analysis of migrants, the United Nations further recommends that migrants only be counted as "long-term migrants" if they are living in or having the intention of living in the host country (outside of their home country) for more than one year.[9] Rather than giving great attention to those who move internally, this book will focus on those who migrate across international borders.

In like manner, *migration* is the "movement of persons away from their place of usual residence, either across an international border or within a State."[10] Once again, this book draws attention to the movement across international borders. It will reveal principles for mission ministry to those who have relocated to another country.

There are two key terms related to the countries involved in the migration process. *Country of origin* (also referred to as *source country*) is "a country of nationality or of former habitual residence of a person or group of persons who have migrated abroad, irrespective of whether they migrate regularly or irregularly."[11] This is the country from which a person migrates.

Meanwhile, the *country of destination* (also known as *host country*) is "a country that is the destination for a person or a group of persons, irrespective of whether they migrate regularly or irregularly."[12] This, then, is the country to which a person migrates.

---

8. Sironi et al., *Glossary on Migration*, 130.
9. United Nations, *Recommendations on Statistics of International Migration*, 5–7.
10. Sironi et al., *Glossary on Migration*, 135.
11. Sironi et al., *Glossary on Migration*, 37.
12. Sironi et al., *Glossary on Migration*, 37.

Sharpening Contemporary Focus on a Timeless Phenomenon

As a migrant moves outside of his/her national borders, he/she is initially recognized as an alien. An *alien* is "an individual who does not have the nationality of the State in whose territory that individual is present."[13] As will be seen in chapter 3, this is also a common English translation of the Hebrew word *ger*, about whom God gave the Israelites clear instruction.

These aliens are often referred to with one of two terms that describe their status within their new state. A *legal migrant* (also called *regular migrant*) is "a person who moves or has moved across an international border and is authorized to enter or to stay in a State pursuant to the law of that State and to international agreements to which that State is a party."[14] Such migrants have the necessary documentation and/or permits allowing them residence (temporary or permanent) in the destination country.

While some are authorized to enter or stay, not all have that status. Although sometimes identified with the with the label *illegal aliens*, literature more often refers to these same people as *irregular* or *undocumented migrants*. These terms describe "a person who moves or has moved across an international border and is not authorized to enter or to stay in a State pursuant to the law of that State and to international agreements to which that State is a party."[15] This refers to both those individuals entering without documentation as well as those who have remained beyond the terms of their legal stay. In fact, Amstutz suggests that roughly 40 percent of irregular migrants in the United States are those who have overstayed their visas.[16]

A *refugee* is a specific type of migrant. He or she is a

> person who, owing to a well-founded fear of persecution for reasons of race, religion, nationality, membership of a particular social group or political opinion, is outside the country of his nationality and is unable or, owing to such fear, is unwilling to avail himself of the protection of that country; or who, not having a nationality and being outside the country of his former habitual residence as a result of such events, is unable or, owing to such fear, is unwilling to return to it.[17]

---

13. Sironi et al., *Glossary on Migration*, 6.
14. Sironi et al., *Glossary on Migration*, 132.
15. Sironi et al., *Glossary on Migration*, 131.
16. Amstutz, *Just Immigration*, 62.
17. Sironi et al., *Glossary on Migration*, 169.

The United Nations High Commissioner on Refugees estimated that there were 25.9 million refugees in 2018.[18]

Some refugees are vetted and invited by host countries to come. Thus, upon arrival, they are granted asylum along with the appropriate documentation and legal residence upon arrival. Other refugees, however, flee from their country of origin and enter a destination country, where they request and apply for asylum. In either case, *asylum* must, ultimately, be granted by the state. It is "protection on its territory to persons outside their country of nationality or habitual residence, who are fleeing persecution or serious harm or for other reasons."[19]

Many migrants seek a long-term, official standing with their new state of residence. They become a *citizen* or *national*, "a person having a legal bond with a State."[20] As such, they possess rights that typically give them access to things like employment opportunities, residency, and voting privileges.

The process of becoming a national citizen in their new host country is called *naturalization*. The International Organization for Migration defines it as "any mode of acquisition after birth of a nationality not previously held by the person that requires an application by this person or his or her legal agent as well as an act of granting nationality by a public authority."[21] In most instances, naturalization is a process requiring the migrant to understand the state's history and laws and to demonstrate facility in the language. (This will be explored further in chapter 8.)

At times, migrants have better income and employment options than loved ones back in their country of origin. In such instances, many choose to send a portion of their income to others. These *remittances* are "private international monetary transfers that migrants make, individually or collectively."[22]

One must exercise caution with such a vocabulary list. Terms and statistics referring to people can be dangerous things. They can depersonalize the realities. Behind the categorizations of people and the numerical estimates are real individuals living in specific life situations. Each of these is a person bearing the image of God. Each one is a person the Father yearns to redeem (2 Pet 3:9).

---

18. UN High Commissioner for Refugees, *Global Trends: 2018*, 2.
19. Sironi et al., *Glossary on Migration*, 11.
20. Sironi et al., *Glossary on Migration*, 141.
21. Sironi et al., *Glossary on Migration*, 143.
22. Sironi et al., *Glossary on Migration*, 178.

Sharpening Contemporary Focus on a Timeless Phenomenon

Meeting the Modern Migrant

If you were to meet today's "median migrant," who would that person be? In broad strokes, you could picture a forty-year-old male from India who is currently living in the United States. Of course, that statistically based caricature is far too generalized. That profile fails to describe reality far more than it portrays it.

Still, who are these men, women, and children? What are their countries of origin? To what countries are they heading? A closer look at the data offers better insight.

Migrant Age

Migrants are not defined by a narrow age demographic. From newborns to senior citizens, these quarter of a billion people span the full spectrum of age. The average age of the migrant population is older than that of the world population. The median age for migrants is thirty-nine.[23] Meanwhile, the median age for world population is thirty.[24]

Migrant Gender

Migrant gender statistics are only somewhat different from those of the world population. Among migrants, the scales tip slightly stronger in favor of a male majority than that of all global residence. The UN reported in 2017 that 51.6 percent of refugees are men.[25] Meanwhile, the current worldwide population, though still favoring males, is comprised of 50.4 percent men.[26]

Migrant Geography

Beyond age and gender, geography is ultimately the defining feature of the migrant experience. After all, according to the definition used earlier, a migrant is a person who "moves away from his or her usual place of

---

23. Vidal and Tjaden, *Global Migration Indicators 2018*, 21.
24. Worldometer, "World Demographics (2020)."
25. UN Department of Economic and Social Affairs, "International Migrant Stock: The 2017 Revision."
26. Worldometer, "World Demographics (2020)."

residence."[27] From where are migrants moving? To what destinations are they going? Migrational direction is a very fluid reality that changes with time. Haas et al. write, "In 1960 more than three quarter of all international migrants who moved to another world region were Europeans. This proportion had shrunk to 22 percent by 2017." Table 1.1 depicts 2017 migration statistics according to continent.

Continent	Migrants living in	Migrants coming from
Asia	80 million	100 million
Europe	78 million	64 million
North America	58 million	5 million
Africa	25 million	38 million
Latin America and Caribbean	20 million	39 million
Oceania	8 million	2 million

Table 1.1. Migration According to Continent in 2017[28]

In the end, however, migration is not a continental phenomenon. It is a national one. It involves a movement from one country to another. At the same time, countries are never exclusively a country of origin or a destination country. In the words of Haas et al., "It is difficult to crunch countries into categories of 'sending' and 'receiving' countries: many countries are both."[29] The United Kingdom serves as a good example of this reality. While the UK hosts 8.8 million migrants, nearly five million people from the UK live in other countries.

Measuring the leading migration host and source countries can be done in two different ways. It is logical to measure sheer total numbers of migrants in or emigrants from specific countries. The United States is the leading host country to migrants with more than four times the number of migrants than the next closest countries of Saudi Arabia, Germany, and

27. Vidal and Tjaden, *Global Migration Indicators 2018*, 130.
28. Vidal and Tjaden, *Global Migration Indicators 2018*, 21.
29. Haas et al., *Age of Migration*, 7.

Sharpening Contemporary Focus on a Timeless Phenomenon

the Russian Federation. Meanwhile, countries like India, Mexico, the Russian Federation, and China are the leading source countries from a purely statistical standpoint.

Host Country	Number of Immigrants
United States	49.8
Saudi Arabia	12.2
Germany	12.2
Russian Federation	11.7
United Kingdom	8.8
United Arab Emirates	8.3
France	7.9
Canada	7.9
Australia	7.0
Spain	5.9

Table 1.2. Top Ten Immigrant Host Countries in 2017 (Millions of Immigrants)[30]

Source Country	Number of Emigrants
India	16.6
Mexico	13.0
Russian Federation	10.6
China	10.0

30. UN Department of Economic and Social Affairs, *International Migration Report 2017*, 6.

Source Country	Number of Emigrants
Bangladesh	7.5
Syrian Arab Republic	6.9
Pakistan	6.0
Ukraine	5.9
Philippines	5.7
United Kingdom	4.9

Table 1.3. Top Ten Immigrant Source Countries in 2017 (Millions of Emigrants)[31]

At the same time, measuring these numbers in terms of percentages of total population in the respective countries can also be very meaningful. This measurement recognizes that a relatively small country can be deeply impacted by even modest movements of people. Using this comparative approach, the perspective of leading host and source countries changes significantly. The only leading host country to appear on both lists is the United Arab Emirates.

In short, a nearly equal proportion of men and women have moved from their country of birth to a new country. Although largely represented by people in the prime of their working years,[32] these individuals span the age range from babies to senior adults. Collectively, they have traveled from every world region and to every world region.

Appreciating Present-Day Push and Pull Factors of Movement

As demonstrated, then, a significant portion of the world population (3 percent) have left their homeland to live in a new country. What is it that has

---

31. UN Department of Economic and Social Affairs, *International Migration Report 2017*, 13.

32. The International Migration Report indicates: "In 2017, 74 percent of all international migrants were age 20 to 64." UN Department of Economic and Social Affairs, *International Migration Report 2017*, 17.

prompted nearly one in thirty people to uproot and go to a new location? The magnetic pull must be strong, causing them to often leave behind their family and the familiar. It must be a powerful push that launches them, at times, into a culture that is often vastly different, frequently comprised of people who think and speak differently.

Beyond this simplistic explanation of the motivations for migration, there are those that are more frequently verbalized. People typically migrate because of economic, educational, political, religious, security, relational, geographic, and climactic realities and opportunities. Still, even these reasons are complex. Often, there is no single motivation. Anthropologists and migration experts have developed theories that explain migration. Many categorize these theories into three different levels. Wickramasinghe and Wimalaratana summarize these categories like this:

> Micro-level theories consider migration decisions from an individual's perspective, i.e. a person's desires and expectations. Macro-level theories consider migration decisions from an aggregate point of view, i.e. the economic structure of the country. Meso-level is where migration decisions lie in between the two former theories, i.e. family bonds, social networks, peer groups and isolated minority communities.[33]

The lines that follow examine some of the reasons for relocation that are often associated with micro theories.

Inspiration and Ability

Before exploring some of these more obvious contributors to human migration, one must acknowledge two contemporary realities that are so simple that they are easily overlooked. In the end, people migrate because they want to and because they can. Growing global awareness inspires many to dream of life elsewhere. Ease of travel makes that dream possible.

There is no doubt that the invention of television and the advent of the Internet and social media have changed the world. The earth has indeed become a global community. Reports of events that may have never reached beyond their local borders or that may have required days to reach other pockets of population are now circulated around the world within minutes. Programs, videos, and information about travel create an international

33. Wickramasinghe and Wimalaratana, "International Migration and Migration Theories," 18.

curiosity about other peoples and places. *HuffPost*, for example, describes the programming of the Travel Channel as "a place for consumers to experience content that gives them access to the world, shared human connections, and engaging talent who celebrate the surprising encounters that happen around the corner and around the globe."[34] As a result, people get a glimpse of other locations and cultures, and the rest of the world seems less "foreign" and more inviting.

Simultaneously, ease of travel has made the world more accessible. In the decade between 2006 and 2015, there was increase in total vehicles in use from 927 million to 1.282 billion.[35] Until the recent COVID-19 pandemic, air travel was also an increasingly used mode of transportation. There were an estimated 4.1 billion airline passengers in 2017,[36] while those at the International Air Transport Association estimate that number will double by 2037.[37] In addition, the total world rail network was expected to increase by 80,000 miles from 2015 to 2020.[38] That is enough for a person to travel more than three times around the world. Rosen writes, "As people continue to migrate to cities for economic opportunity, the middle class will expand—and begin to travel, particularly within the developing bloc of Brazil, Russia, India, and China (BRIC) . . . business and leisure travel is growing faster there than in developed countries."[39]

It is not likely that many modern migrants consciously consider global awareness and ease of travel to be reasons for their movement. Still, global awareness makes migration imaginable. In like manner, ease of travel makes migration possible.[40]

---

34. "Travel Channel."

35. Statista, "Number of Vehicles in Use Worldwide."

36. This is not the number of unique passengers. Rather, it reflects an estimate of total flights taken. Rosen, "Over 4 Billion Passengers Flew in 2017."

37. At the writing of this book, the long-term impact of COVID-19 on travel is unclear. The data cited was extracted from "Passenger Numbers to Hit 8.2bn by 2037."

38. Statista, "Length of the World's Railway Networks."

39. Rosen, "As Billions More Fly."

40. It should also be noted that many, especially those whose lives and basic needs are threatened, often take desperate and dangerous steps in pursuit of safety and provision. Their travel experience is anything but "easy." Many an asylum seeker has experienced peril and even loss of life while traveling in crowded rubber rafts on the tempest-tossed Mediterranean or while being concealed in containers in hopes of being crossing borders to safety. Similarly, many are those who attempt to walk days in hot climates and through rugged terrain in hopes of crossing a border at a location that is not patrolled.

Sharpening Contemporary Focus on a Timeless Phenomenon

Economic/Labor

Employment opportunities are not equally distributed around the world. Similarly, compensation for employment differs significantly within countries and between countries. As global awareness grows, people are also becoming increasingly aware of better and less costly health care options in other locations. Castelli writes, "Poor health services, little educated and qualified work force and poverty are a fertile background promoting migration of individuals in search of better life."[41]

Family Migration

Although the data is sparse on this important factor for migration,[42] the experience is common. In fact, the OECD (Organisation for Economic Co-operation and Development)[43] reports that family migration accounted "for around 40 percent of new permanent migrants in OECD countries in 2017." This organization goes on to describe family migration as the "most important migration channel" in member countries.[44]

Family migration is a broad term that encompasses four different categories of migration. Once again, the OECD identifies and defines these terms. *Family formation* is one aspect of family migration. This describes the scenario when "a resident national or foreigner marries a foreigner and sponsors that individual for admission or for status change." *Accompanying family* is a second category of family migration where "family members are admitted together with the principal migrant." A third type of family migration is *family reunification*. Often in the news, this describes the situation when "family members migrate after the arrival of the principal migrant who sponsors their admission. The family ties predate the arrival of the principal migrant." The final category of family migration is *international adoption*, where "a resident national or foreigner adopts a child of foreign

---

41. Castelli, "Drivers of Migration," 3.

42. Migration Data Portal, "Family Migration."

43. The OECD is comprised of "34 member countries that discuss and develop economic and social policy." Kenton, "Organisation for Economic Co-Operation and Development."

44. Organisation for Economic Co-operation and Development, *International Migration Outlook 2019*, executive summary.

nationality resident abroad."⁴⁵ Thus family migration is one of the primary reasons people move.

Education/Study

Each year, millions of students choose to study in countries outside of their own. Based on interviews with hundreds of students, Quacquarelli Symonds, an organization that ranks universities, indicates the top five reasons students study abroad. Employment prospects as a result of international experience was the number one motivator. In addition, students appreciate the worldwide connections and quality of education that are part of their experience. Finally, the cross-cultural student experience and opportunity to travel round out these key motivators.⁴⁶

The primary host countries to students studying abroad include the United States, United Kingdom, Australia, France, Germany, and the Russian Federation. These students come from countries like China, India, Germany, South Korea, Nigeria, France, and Saudi Arabia. In 2017, UNESCO reported 5.3 million international students.⁴⁷ This represents just over 2 percent of the total migrant stock.

Persecution/Safety

Over 10 percent of the 258 million total migrants are refugees. According to a 2018 report from the United Nations High Commissioner on Refugees, there were a total 25.9 million refugee men, women, and children.⁴⁸ Syria was the leading source country with nearly seven million people who have fled due to the civil war that has been waged for years. Afghanistan, with more than 2.5 million refugees in flight, represented the second leading source country as people have responded and continue to respond to more than three decades of conflict. South Sudan, also with well over two million refugees, was the third dominant country of origin.⁴⁹

---

45. Kenton, "Organisation for Economic Co-Operation and Development."
46. Karzunina, "Why Do Students Want to Study Abroad?"
47. Quacquarelli Symonds is an organization that ranks universities worldwide. "Education: Outbound Internationally Mobile Students."
48. UN High Commissioner for Refugees, *Global Trends: 2018*, 2.
49. UN High Commissioner for Refugees, *Global Trends: 2018*, 14, 15.

Sharpening Contemporary Focus on a Timeless Phenomenon

Of course, refugees are not only fleeing from a location of risk. They are also fleeing to a location of hope—a place where they hope to experience safety and protection. Turkey is, by far, the most welcoming of countries as measured by sheer number of refugees in the country. Germany, meanwhile, is the only country that appears in both lists of top host countries to migrants in general and to refugees specifically.[50]

Climate/Natural Disaster

As a result of a December 26, 2004 tsunami, more than 270,000 people from eleven different countries lost their lives. On April 25, 2015, an earthquake shook portions of Nepal, killing nearly nine thousand people.[51] Meanwhile, the BBC reported in October of 2018, "Nearly nine hundred people are known to have been killed by Hurricane Matthew in Haiti, with aid officials saying up to ninety percent of some areas have been destroyed."[52]

The most obvious and tragic statistics from any natural disaster are those counting the loss of life and the price tag of rebuilding. Less apparent, however, is the fact that people are often forced from their homes. The Internal Displacement Monitoring Center reports nearly nineteen million were displaced in 2017 alone as a result of things like drought, storms, floods, hurricanes, earthquakes, and tsunamis.[53] While it is true that many of these people migrate internally to other locations within the same nation, such disasters also result in international migration.

At the same time, climate change is often cited as a reality that will have an ever-increasing impact on migration. The UN International Organization for Migration estimates a minimum of two hundred million migrants as a result of climate change by 2050.[54] Others, like de Haas et al., consider these estimates to be exaggerated.[55] Regardless of the actual numbers, it seems clear that climate realities have impacted and will continue to impact people's decision to migrate. International response to those fleeing

---

50. UN High Commissioner for Refugees, *Global Trends: 2018*, 17–20.
51. "Nepal Earthquake."
52. "Storm-Hit Haiti Areas '90% Destroyed.'"
53. Internal Displacement Monitoring Centre, "Global Internal Displacement Database."
54. Brown, *Migration and Climate Change*, 21–30.
55. Haas et al., *Age of Migration*, 36–40.

because of climate change is complicated by the fact that these migrants do not fit into internationally recognized refugee frameworks.

Because of the realities of these natural disaster and climate issues, the United Nations included this topic in their recently adopted *Global Compact for Safe, Orderly, and Regular Migration*. The second objective listed in this document addresses "natural disasters, the adverse effects of climate change, and environmental degradation." Their goal is to "minimize the adverse drivers and structural factors that compel people to leave their country of origin."[56]

Together, all of the above influences (and others to be explored later) have contributed to the movement of 3 percent of the world population from their "place of usual residence . . . across an international border."[57] These factors describe some of the reasons a Syrian family may now reside in Germany. They lend understanding to the presence of a Chinese international student at the university nearby. They offer insight on how a Polish construction worker is employed in the Netherlands or how a Turkish family member seeks to unite with others in France. These realities help to explain why men, women, and children from Indonesia fled suddenly to other countries in 2004 after the tsunami.

Capturing Current Global Interest

If it is true that migration rates have remained relatively constant, how is it, then, that migration has, in recent years, attracted such widespread public attention? Whether it is a terrorist attack presumably caused by a migrant, a migrant convoy headed towards a border, the latest legislation limiting or granting greater access to potential migrants, migrants fleeing from civil war or countries welcoming refugees, migration realities are communicated like never before. Certainly, the global awareness mentioned earlier allows wider-spread public insight into what had been a less public phenomenon. Still, the broader attention is progressively more rooted in increased politicization of migration.

The term *politicization* can have a negative overtone. That is not necessarily implied in its use here. In many regards, migration has always been a political issue—and it should be. As the Scriptures demonstrate and chapter

---

56. Global Compact for Migration, *Global Compact for Safe, Orderly*, 8, 9.
57. Sironi et al., *Glossary on Migration*, 130.

Sharpening Contemporary Focus on a Timeless Phenomenon

6 outlines, God has given to the state the responsibility to establish laws and policy for the welfare of its citizens (Rom 13:1–7).

The development of proper migration laws and policies is critical since migration represents a powerful influence. The International Organization for Migration expresses it well:

> Migration can be a constructive economic and social force, bringing about a dynamic labour force, economy and community, and rich cultural diversity . . . But migration can also have negative consequences and associations: trafficking and smuggling, irregular migration, security, and xenophobia and racism . . . As societies become more and more affected by migration, the central challenge is how to manage migration to maximize its positive effects and minimize potentially negative results. States are increasingly looking to migration management to reap the potential gains of migration without incurring too many of its potential costs.[58]

But the task of maximizing the positive effects and minimizing the negative results of migration is not a simple one. There is no lack of differing opinions on how to accomplish those twin goals. Certainly, there are genuine challenges faced by both source countries and host countries. The realities of rampant irregular migration and widespread fear of terrorism must be addressed. Data related to irregular migrants is difficult to produce since these individuals are, by definition, not documented. Still, even estimates demonstrate that irregular migrants are not only numerous but ubiquitous. EU estimates in 2008 (before the Syrian refugee crisis) ranged from 1.9 to 3.8 million.[59] In the United States, there were an estimated 10.5 million irregular migrants.[60] The Russian Federation estimated having between five and six million irregular migrant workers in 2011. The United Nations reported in 2013 that "irregular migration was a major concern for Governments of twenty-two of the twenty-five countries with the largest migrant stocks, and for Governments of sixteen of the twenty-five countries with the highest percentages of migrants in the total population."[61] In that regard, then, irregular migration requires political attention.

---

58. International Organization for Migration, *World Migration Report 2003*, 52.
59. Irregular Migration, "Irregular-Migration: Stock Estimates."
60. Krogstad et al., "Key Facts about Illegal Immigration in the U.S."
61. UN Department of Economic and Social Affairs, *International Migration Policies*, 92.

Concerns about migration are much broader than merely knowing who is residing within national boundaries and whether they are legally permitted to do so. For many, migration is also linked with issues of security and acts of terrorism. These and other issues related to immigration policy and perception will be the focus of chapters 4 and 5.

Focusing Modern Missional Emphasis

Even though migration itself is not a new development, the wider-spread recognition of the corresponding missional opportunity and responsibility is. In 1974, respected author and missiologist Ralph Winter anticipated the looming need to give theological and methodological focus to this important area. Sadiri Joy Tira recalls personal conversations with Winter in that year and again later in 1989. Tira reports that he shared, "The world has changed. The Unreached People Groups are now scattered all over the world . . . Your generation will have to deal with mass migration and globalization."[62]

Indeed, global missional efforts were once largely characterized by the migration of the missionary to the relatively stationary unreached in their respective national and cultural contexts. Today, missiologists and practitioners must now recognize Winter's words as prophetic. Many individual believers, missional churches, and mission agencies are recognizing the opportunities afforded by the movements of these people from their countries and cultures. With roughly 258 million people living outside of their countries of origin in 2017,[63] these movements cause Christ followers to recognize their responsibility to love their neighbor as themselves (Luke 10:25–37). Such migration also makes it possible to make disciples among people groups outside of their native contexts. At times, the gospel opportunities afforded in new host countries would not have been possible through traditional missional approaches in their countries of origin where overt missionary work may have been forbidden

---

62. Tira, "Preface," xix.
63. Vidal and Tjaden, *Global Migration Indicators 2018*, 9.

Sharpening Contemporary Focus on a Timeless Phenomenon

Book Outline

This book, then, seeks to communicate key information that will enable followers of Jesus to better understand this timeless but contemporary phenomenon. The reader will explore God's divine purposes in migration, the inherent challenges, and wise mission practices for those that would accept the responsibility and engage the opportunity.

The book is comprised of eight chapters. Chapters 2 and 3 offer theological backdrop for understanding migration. Here, the reader is invited to explore, analyze, and appreciate God's purposes for migration as well as Old Testament guidelines and New Testament examples of migration ministry.

Chapters 4 and 5 analyze different theories of international relations and their impact on migration policy and convictions. Here, the reader will grow to better understand the personal and political tensions associated with immigration. These chapters also encourage the reader to synthesize a biblical response as he/she engages with these realities.

Contextualization and integration are essential ingredients of effective ministry among migrants in a new host country. Differences of language, culture, and religion can make both ministry and inclusion in society and in the local church challenging. Chapter 6 addresses this meshing of people and cultures.

Chapter 7 gives attention to the use of technology in migrant ministry. The COVID-19 pandemic moved technological tools and resources from the fringe to the center of relational engagement and disciple making. This has prompted greater utilization and innovation in their use. Thus, this chapter sketches ways in which some of these digital resources can be utilized for sake of eternity.

The final chapter closes with a theological and practical examination of strategy development. Here, the reader explores biblical cautions about ministry plan development and the ministry "strategies" of Jesus and of the apostle Paul.

As you read this book, may you be inspired and equipped to participate in this great missional opportunity. May the future celebration of the gathering of the nations be even sweeter for you.

> After this I looked, and there before me was a great multitude that no one could count, from every nation, tribe, people and language, standing before the throne and before the Lamb. They were wearing white robes and were holding palm branches in their hands.

That They Might Seek Him

And they cried out in a loud voice: "Salvation belongs to our God, who sits on the throne, and to the Lamb." (Rev 7:9–10)

2

Developing a Theology of Migration

To fourteen-year-old Mehdi, his family's move from Morocco seemed random. It seemed irrational. He just couldn't grasp the reasons that would cause them to uproot. Sure, they had explained the rationale for the move to Turkey, but, still, it was hard to accept.

He had just wrapped up the difficult years of middle school. In his search for acceptance, he had found a few close friends. They spent lots of time together kicking a soccer ball around, and they texted lots when they were apart. Those relationships were about to be disrupted. In Turkey, he would be the odd man out. His Arabic would stand out against their Turkish. He would be the awkward one learning the way to do things in their culture. He would be the one not invited and not included. He would be the one trying to break into the in-crowd—or into any crowd, for that matter.

Mehdi had responded to the news of the imminent move in all of the predictable ways. He had questioned his parents. He had presented his case for staying. He had argued with them—sometimes at high volume. He had acted out in rebellion. None of it seemed to make a difference.

The only thing left to do was to take it up with Allah . . . with God . . . with whomever was up there, if anyone was. He didn't particularly share his parent's Islamic faith. Oh, he went through the motions by being in the right places at the right times, kneeling in the right manner and facing in the right direction, mouthing the right prayers, fasting at Ramadan, and memorizing the beliefs and pillars. But still, he wasn't convinced.

That They Might Seek Him

Nevertheless, he asked this Divine Being to change their minds. And, if it had to be, he asked him to give him understanding. Why migration? Why his family? Why now?

ACADEMICIANS DEEM IT IMPORTANT to investigate the fine details of small facets of areas of studies. Practitioners, meanwhile, may describe these efforts as "getting into the weeds." While the former may justify their research in that they are "expanding knowledge for future application," the latter may joke that their counterparts are "learning more and more about less and less until they know everything about nothing."

How does the development of a theology of migration and migration ministry fit into that banter? It may seem like an unnecessary, perhaps even tedious focus on a relatively small aspect of the broader study of missiology. Is it truly worth the effort? After all, this narrow missional, theological framework fits under the larger umbrella of theology of mission and of the *Missio Dei*. Others have clearly and extensively explored these more comprehensive topics. Has not one adequately considered this particular nuanced slice by examining the whole missional pie in a general fashion?

The Need for Theology of Migration

To the contrary, such a specialized, limited focus on the theology of migration has value for at least two important reasons. First of all, a concentrated examination of this subject is essential because it is reasonably new and relatively untapped in terms of the sheer recognition of the opportunity and its theological undergirding. Missiologists and theologians have only recently begun to explore at a deeper level biblical truths related to this specific topic. Secondly, such a theological understanding of migration is vital because it is theology that should, ultimately, drive strategy development and mission practices among those living outside of their countries of origin. It is when one understands God's purposes in migration that one is best able to serve migrants in ways that most honor and glorify him. These two realities of its new, strategic nature deserve further exploration.

Developing a Theology of Migration

Migration Missiology as New

As stated in chapter 1, people have been on the move from the dawn of creation. Still, even though migration itself is not a new development, the broader recognition of the corresponding missional potential and responsibility is. In 1974, respected author and missiologist Ralph Winter anticipated the looming need to give theological and methodological focus to this important area. Sadiri Joy Tira recalls personal conversations with Winter in that year and again later in 1989. Tira reports that he shared, "The world has changed. The Unreached People Groups are now scattered all over the world . . . Your generation will have to deal with mass migration and globalization."[1]

Indeed, missiologists and practitioners must now recognize Winter's words as prophetic. With roughly 258 million people living outside of their countries of origin in 2017,[2] migration has captured the attention of believers and unbelievers alike. Many are writing about it and individuals, churches, and mission agencies have begun to recognize that migration is bringing the unreached within reach. Samuel Escobar was one of the earliest to specifically address the missiological challenges and opportunities represented by this movement in his 2003 article "Migration: Avenue and Challenge to Mission."[3] He recognized that such theological reflection about this nuanced branch of mission is critical.

The Lausanne Movement, known for its desire to "connect influencers and ideas for global mission," has given concentrated focus to "diaspora missiology" over the last fifteen years. As a result, many good resources have been made available. The *New People Next Door*, written in 2004 by Tom Houston et al., was one of their earliest works. This book traces biblical records of diaspora movements, examines some specific people groups on the move, and provides projections for this growing reality in the coming decades.[4]

In 2009, mission leaders at the Lausanne Diaspora Educators Consultation developed "The Seoul Declaration on Diaspora Missiology." Although the purpose of this Lausanne resource is not to outline a theology of migration ministry, it does identify God's sovereignty in the movement of

---

1. Tira, "Preface," xix.
2. Vidal and Tjaden, *Global Migration Indicators 2018*, 9.
3. Escobar, "Migration: Avenue and Challenge to Mission," 17–28.
4. Houston et al., *New People Next Door*.

people and the need to practice diaspora missions in a biblically informed way. It also urges churches, mission agencies, leaders, and individuals to engage with this unique opportunity.[5] Since then, the Lausanne Movement has formed the Global Diaspora Network to give even greater focused attention to ministry among people on the move.

But the Lausanne Movement is not alone. Others are studying this phenomenon. Perhaps the most widely circulated of recent books on the subject is J. D. Payne's 2012 work entitled *Strangers Next Door*. In the book, Payne traces the terms, history, and theology of migration ministry while offering some general strategic insights.[6] Meanwhile, people like Enoch Wan have been prolific in research, writing, and editing of materials on this important subject.[7] Indeed, reaching nations on the move has captured the attention and imagination of many over the last several decades.

Migration Missiology as Strategically Essential

The development of migration theology is also critical for fruitful migration ministry. Gailyn Van Rheenen reminds practitioners that strategy development for mission ministry is best when it is rooted in theological reflection, cultural analysis, and historical perspective.[8] With regard to theological reflection, descriptive and prescriptive Bible truths must be weighed in an attempt to understand God's plans for such ministry. Elliston describes well the importance of the theological component in missiological research. He writes, "Mission theology is at its best when it is intimately involved in the being, knowing, doing, and serving of the Church's mission in a particular context."[9]

Thus, migration missiology is a new discipline with strategic implications. Theologians and practitioners alike must recognize the importance and prevalence of biblical truth that should drive the mission of fruitful and passionate outreach among those on the move. While drawing heavily from the Word of God and relatively recent scholarship of others, this

---

5. Lausanne Diaspora Educators Consultation, "Seoul Declaration on Diaspora Missiology."

6. Payne, *Strangers Next Door*.

7. Some of these resources can be viewed at http://www.enochwan.com/.

8. Van Rheenen, "MR #26: The Missional Helix."

9. Elliston, *Introduction to Missiological Research Design*, 118.

chapter paints a biblical/theological backdrop to this relatively untapped area of missional fascination and opportunity.

A Biblical/Systematic Approach

There are multiple ways that one might engage in the development of a theology of migration. Theological methodologies are often described in terms of their specific approach. *Biblical* theology is one of those approaches. This is a specific method in which the theologian attempts to trace theological development as outlined in specific books of the Bible and over the course of eras of time. Charles Ryrie describes biblical theology as "that branch of theological science which deals systematically with the historically conditioned progress of the self-revelation of God as deposited in the Bible."[10]

Historical theology is another approach to theological study. Those using this method attempt to trace what people have believed throughout history. Paul Enns says that historical theology "attempts to understand the formation of the doctrines, their development and change—for better or worse."[11] So, whereas biblical theology focuses on what God has revealed over time, historical theology looks at what people have believed over time.

Systematic theology is another theological grid for understanding Scripture. It is typically known for its present-day attempt, its topical approach, and its whole-Bible focus. Unlike biblical theology, systematic theology does not attempt to trace the historical developments of God's revelation. Grudem states, "Systematic theology involves collecting and understanding all the relevant passages in the Bible on various topics and then summarizing their teachings clearly so that we know what to believe about each topic."[12]

Dogmatic theology is yet another approach to expressing biblical truth. Dogmatic theology is much like systematic theology, but it is typically adopted by a church, denomination, or ecclesiastical body. Enns contrasts the two like this:

> Many systematic theologies have been written without the official sanction or endorsement of a church or ecclesiastical body. Dogmatic theology discusses the same doctrines and normally in

---

10. Ryrie, *Biblical Theology of the New Testament*, 44.
11. Enns, *Moody Handbook of Theology*, 433.
12. Grudem, *Systematic Theology*, 21.

the same outline and manner as systematic theology, but from a particular theological stand and church identification.[13]

Which theological approach best serves an attempt to understand migration? This chapter outlines biblical teaching on migration from the standpoint of both biblical and systematic theology. In other words, there will be the attempt to outline both God's unfolding use of migration over the course of time as well as a comprehensive perspective that encompasses God's revealed purposes for migration. These two approaches are intermingled without an attempt to distinguish which theological grid is being used at a specific time.

Key Contours to Migration Theology

The missional heart of God is not exclusive to either testament of the Bible. Both point to the reality of human depravity (Rom 5:12–21). Both reverberate with christological centrality (Luke 24:25–27). Both outline a sense of missional responsibility to the nations as the Old Testament speaks of the blessing of the "families of the earth" (Gen 12:1–3) and the New Testament describes the church's responsibility to "make disciples of all the nations" (Matt 28:18–20).

Migration has played an instrumental role in this missional process. Through migration, nations are formed. God has also used migration to punish and correct people and nations. In addition, migration has been a means used by God as he has provided for and protected people. Ultimately, however, the Father has demonstrated redemptive purposes in migration. These Old and New Testament realities are outlined in the lines that follow.

Migration and the Formation of the Nations

Genesis 10 and 11 contain the first biblical references to the nations. The "Table of Nations" outlined in Genesis 10 describes the descendants of Japheth, Ham, and Shem and the formation of nations from these sons of Noah. How did this come about? The biblical author points to people with genealogical connections and shared languages who migrated (the NASB uses the terms "separated," from the Hebrew *parad* in 10:5 and 10:32, and "spread," from the Hebrew *puwts* in 10:18) to different lands. Although one

---

13. Enns, *Moody Handbook of Theology*, 500.

Developing a Theology of Migration

chapter later, Genesis 11 actually takes a chronological step backward to outline the process used by God in the formation of these nations.[14] The confusing of the languages led people to gather linguistically and move together. This migration resulted in the formation of the nations.

The nation of Israel is among those formed by migration. As just described, description of the nations and their territories and the events of Babel that led to their scattering serve as the backdrop for God's selection and direction of Abraham. With those realities in mind, Terah set out with his family from Ur headed towards Canaan. After his death, God introduced the Abrahamic covenant. This covenant promised the formation of a nation comprised of Abraham's offspring, who would inhabit a specific land and who would be a source of blessing/cursing to the other families (Gen 11:31—12:3). Hebrews 11 described the resultant migration of Abraham and his family: "By faith Abraham, when he was called, obeyed by going out to a place which he was to receive for an inheritance; and he went out not knowing where he was going" (Heb 11:8). Thus, God used migration in the establishment of his chosen nation.

Even though the realities of the formation of the nations first become clear in Genesis 10–12, the Lord's plan to use of migration in this way unfolded as early as the first chapter of Genesis. In that regard, his intention for the nations or *ethne* of the world[15] was neither a post-deluge revelation nor a sheer impromptu, necessary response to the pride of humankind at Babel. It was in the garden of Eden that God gave what Nehrbass and others describe as a "cultural mandate" to Adam and Eve.[16] He instructed these parents of the human race to "be fruitful and increase in number; fill the earth and subdue it. Rule over the fish in the sea and the birds in the sky and over every living creature that moves on the ground" (Gen 1:28). This filling of the earth required the migration of humankind. Thus, in the words of Rodas, "geographic movement is part of what it means to be human."[17] Since, then, God's plan expressed both a divine image bearing

---

14. The prideful desire of man to stay together, build a tower to heaven, and to "make a name for ourselves" caused God to confuse their languages, resulting in their scattering and the formation of the nations (Gen 11:1–9).

15. Although "nations" will be further defined later in this chapter in terms of words like *ethne*, it will be used throughout as a reference to ethnic groups, not to geographical/political entities. This usage is much the same as that found in Piper, *Let the Nations Be Glad*, 179.

16. Nehrbass, *God's Image and Global Cultures*, 66, 67.

17. Carroll R., "Diaspora and Mission in the Old Testament," 102.

and a cultural mandate, Van Til's description of paradise (the garden of Eden) as "the beginning of the cultural world"[18] is fitting. God's plan was that migration and cultural-ethnic development would go hand in hand.

From the point of creation, God revealed his heart to share a relationship with men and women who were to inhabit the entire earth. Not only does this reference to filling the earth offer the first hint of the nations, but it also gives insight into God's use of migration to populate the earth and form them. Wan indicates, "It was God's design that humankind should scatter. Scattering was actually a blessing from Jehovah before the fall."[19] Although migration is, at times, spawned by sinful acts of oppression and war, it was part of the Father's original intentions for people made in his image. Thus, Genesis 1:26–28 (repeated in part in Genesis 9:7) may be seen as more than a "cultural mandate." It is also a "migration mandate" that has led to the formation of the nations.

Migration and the Punishment and Correction of People

In addition to giving the cultural/migrational mandate to humankind, God also gave Adam and Eve other responsibilities, freedoms, and restrictions. Genesis 2:15–16 describes these.

> Then the LORD God took the man and put him into the garden of Eden to cultivate it and keep it. The LORD God commanded the man, saying, "From any tree of the garden you may eat freely; but from the tree of the knowledge of good and evil you shall not eat, for in the day that you eat from it you will surely die."

It was Adam's responsibility to cultivate and keep the garden. He was given freedom and restriction in regard to his diet.

Violating the restriction would have its consequences—death, both physical and spiritual.[20] In addition, their violation in Genesis 3 had implications for the serpent, the man, and the woman. But there was one more punitive consequence to Adam and Eve's violation of God's plan. The pair was driven from the garden. God forced them to migrate, preventing access

---

18. Van Til, *Calvinistic Concept of Culture*, 139.

19. Wan, "Diachronic Overview of Christian Missions," 164.

20. In the genealogy of Genesis 5, the repeated phrase "and then he died" serves as a real reminder of the physical consequences of Adam's choice. Similarly, the reality of spiritual death is expressed clearly in the words "you were dead in your trespasses and sins" in Eph 2:1.

Developing a Theology of Migration

to the garden and the eating from the tree of life (Gen 3:22–24). This first example of human migration, then, is one of many in which God used migration as a means of retribution or correction.

Though it was mentioned earlier, the judgment at Babel (Gen 11:1–9) is another illustration of God's use of migration as a form of punishment. It is true, the confusion of languages and resultant scattering accomplished God's purpose in the formation of the nations. Still, the Father also used it as a punitive measure in response to humankind's cooperative, prideful efforts and misguided worship. It served as a preventative means of curbing the depths of man's independent, sinful efforts.

Certainly, many other instances of God's punitive, corrective use of migration can be cited. Among the more familiar examples are the exile experiences of both Israel and Judah. One dare not overlook the backdrop for these migratory movements. After the reign of Solomon over the united kingdom of Israel, the Jews rallied around two separate leaders and divided along tribal lines into two separate kingdoms. For the generations that followed, the ten northern tribes were like a separate nation with their own kings. They retained the name Israel. Meanwhile, two southern tribes were named after the more prominent tribe, Judah. Judah also had its rulers.

Each of these kingdoms rebelled against God. As a result, God brought punishment on them in the form of migrational exile. For the kingdom of Israel, God used the Assyrians. The book of 2 Kings described it in this way:

> In the ninth year of Hoshea, the king of Assyria captured Samaria and carried Israel away into exile to Assyria, and settled them in Halah and Habor, *on* the river of Gozan, and in the cities of the Medes.
> Now *this* came about because the sons of Israel had sinned against the LORD their God, who had brought them up from the land of Egypt from under the hand of Pharaoh, king of Egypt, and they had feared other gods and walked in the customs of the nations whom the LORD had driven out before the sons of Israel (2 Kgs 17:6–8a)

"Exile," translated from the Hebrew *galah*, is often associated with forced exile. Santos indicates that it "may have become a specialized term later in the nation's history to mean 'to be taken into exile,' when deportations of whole population groups as a means of conquest entered into Israel's history."[21]

---

21. Santos, "Exploring the Major Dispersion Terms and Realities," 37.

Judah's story of migration is similar. Although these southern tribes were, at times, privileged to have godly kings leading them, they also strayed from their Creator. As a result, God used a godless nation to bring desolation to Jerusalem. Many from Judah were also taken from their homeland in forced migration to Babylon. Jeremiah predicted this in his writings.

> Therefore thus says the LORD of hosts, "Because you have not obeyed My words, behold,
> I will send and take all the families of the north," declares the LORD, "and *I will send* to Nebuchadnezzar king of Babylon, My servant, and will bring them against this land and against its inhabitants and against all these nations round about; and I will utterly destroy them and make them a horror and a hissing, and an everlasting desolation. Moreover, I will take from them the voice of joy and the voice of gladness, the voice of the bridegroom and the voice of the bride, the sound of the millstones and the light of the lamp. This whole land will be a desolation and a horror, and these nations will serve the king of Babylon seventy years." (Jer 25:8–11)

In summary of the Babylonian and Assyrian exiles, Santos writes, "The Lord's judgment to lead Israel out of the land into exile functions as a major contrast to his carrying out his promises to give the people the land as a gift at the beginning of their history as a nation."[22]

The God of heaven, then, has used migration punitively. He has done so on both an individual and a group/national level. He has used it as a means of bringing correction and punishment.

Migration as a Means of Provision and Protection

Beyond God's use of migration in the formation and punishment of nations and peoples, the Scriptures also depict his provisional/protective use of the movements of people. This is illustrated in the Old Testament in times when the nation of Israel experienced famine and antagonism. The New Testament, meanwhile, describes the Father's use of migration as a means of protecting his own Son from a premature death.

As Jacob and his sons experienced famine in the Old Testament, sons of Jacob made trips to Egypt to procure grain for food (Gen 43–45). These trips led ultimately to the migratory relocation of the nation of Israel in its early days. At that time, sixty-six men, women, and children made their

---

22. Santos, "Exploring the Major Dispersion Terms and Realities," 37.

Developing a Theology of Migration

way to Egypt (Gen 46:26–27), where they joined Joseph and his family. Thus, provision was made for the people of God.

Meanwhile, some four hundred years later, God used migration to protect his people. Although he had promised them blessing in their own land, they experienced opposition while still located in the land of Egypt. God's plan was to protect and provide for them by bringing them back to the land of promise. Moses played a primary role in leading the people over the next forty years.

Indeed, the journey itself could have been much shorter. Unfortunately, even this example of God's provisional/protective use of migration also had elements of his use of punitive/corrective migration (Num 13–14). After sending spies into the promised land, the people accepted the majority recommendation to not risk going into the land. Consequently, God responded, "And your sons shall be shepherds for forty years in the wilderness, and they shall suffer for your unfaithfulness, until your corpses lie in the wilderness" (Num 14:33).

After the forty years, God's people experienced provision and protection through his use of migration. Under Joshua's leadership, the Israelites entered the land God had given them centuries before. Thus, they were no longer living in bondage as when the nation had been enslaved in Egypt.

The New Testament also provides examples of God's provisional/protective use of migration. One of the more prominent examples is found in the very life of Jesus. In a familiar portion of the traditional Christmas story, Matthew's gospel (Matt 2:1–15) describes the journey of the magi to Jerusalem in search of the man who had been born as king of the Jews. Feeling threatened, Herod invited the magi to return to give a report. In protection, God directed the magi to return by a different route. God also provided protection to his own Son by directing Mary and Joseph to migrate temporarily to Egypt while Herod issued a decree that baby boys two years old and younger be killed.

Thus, the Bible depicts God's use of migration as a means of providing for and protecting people. Readers observe this in Old Testament examples of migration in times of famine and oppression. In the New Testament, God directed magi, Mary, and Joseph to take paths that led to the protection of his Son.

That They Might Seek Him

Migration and the Redemption of the Nations

Beyond God's use of migration in the formation of the nations, the correction and protection of people, the apostle Paul pointed out God's underlying, eternal purposes in the movements of people in his address on Mars Hill. He described it with these words:

> He Himself gives to all *people* life and breath and all things; and He made from one *man* every nation of mankind to live on all the face of the earth, having determined *their* appointed times and the boundaries of their habitation, that they would seek God, if perhaps they might grope for Him and find Him, though He is not far from each one of us; for in Him we live and move and exist (Acts 17:25b–28a).

In other words, God orchestrates the geography and the chronology of people/nations for his redemptive purposes.

This is further borne out in the book of Revelation. There, the apostle John was afforded a look at a yet future gathering of the redeemed. In chapter 7, his observations are described in these words:

> After this I looked, and there before me was a great multitude that no one could count, from every nation, tribe, people and language, standing before the throne and before the Lamb. They were wearing white robes and were holding palm branches in their hands. And they cried out in a loud voice:
> "Salvation belongs to our God, who sits on the throne, and to the Lamb." (Rev 7:9–10)

Thus, the Father's intentional scattering outlined in Genesis ultimately gives rise to a redemptive gathering in Revelation. John uses four terms to describe those gathered. They were "a great multitude . . . from every nation, tribe, people and language." The *Greek-English Lexicon of the New Testament and Other Early Christian Literature* provides definition to the key terms. "Nation" has a meaning different than its "common English usage" as "a political or geographic grouping."[23] "Nation" is the translation of the Greek word *ethnos*, also referring to people, foreigners, pagans, or Gentiles.[24] "Tribe" comes from the word *phyle*, which is also translated as "nation" or "people."[25] "People" is the New American Standard translation

---

23. Piper, *Let the Nations Be Glad*, 183.
24. Bauer and Gingrich, *Greek-English Lexicon*, 218.
25. Bauer and Gingrich, *Greek-English Lexicon*, 868, 869.

Developing a Theology of Migration

of *laos*, which elsewhere refers to people in general, people as a nation, or to the people of God.[26] "Tongue" (*glossa*) also refers to "language."[27]

The distinctions outlined here, then, point to ethnic, cultural, and linguistic differences that are celebrated in eternity. Yes, those gathered are diverse. Their differences stem, at least in part, from the migration of their forefathers, their separation from others, and corresponding cultural-linguistic development. Nevertheless, these men and women from corresponding nations are not defined in terms of governments and geographic boundaries recognized by the United Nations.

These same four terms are also used two chapters earlier in Revelation 5. At that point, four living creatures and twenty-four elders extoled the merits of the Son of God by singing:

> Worthy are You to take the book and to break its seals; for You were slain, and purchased for God with Your blood *men* from every tribe and tongue and people and nation. You have made them *to be* a kingdom and priests to our God; and they will reign upon the earth. (Rev 5:9–10)

In summary of Revelation 5:9–10, Bosch writes, "[here] we see that the work of redemption by the Lamb of God has been proclaimed and received by people from all nations and from every background."[28] Rather than geopolitical entities, these nations, tribes, people, and tongues have recently been referred to as "people groups." The 1982 Lausanne Committee defined a people group as "the largest group within which the Gospel can spread as a church planting movement without encountering barriers of understanding or acceptance."[29] The Joshua Project estimates that there are roughly 17,100 people groups with more than 7,000 still unreached.[30] They further define an "unreached people group" as "a people group among which there is no indigenous community of believing Christians with adequate numbers and resources to evangelize this people group without outside assistance."[31]

These passages in Revelation make it clear that the Son provides redemption for those from every people group. He does so through his blood.

26. Bauer and Gingrich, *Greek-English Lexicon*, 466, 467.
27. Bauer and Gingrich, *Greek-English Lexicon*, 162.
28. Ott et al., *Encountering Theology of Mission*, 5.
29. Joshua Project, "What Is a People Group?"
30. Joshua Project, "Global Statistics."
31. Joshua Project, "Definitions."

This redemption is appropriated only to the "elect from" the nations (Matt 24:31) who believe in him (John 3:16). In his sovereignty, God, then, orchestrates the migration of these nations for his redemptive purposes.

Migration and the Making of Disciples of the Nations

God's first command to humans, then, instructed them to migrate. This migration ultimately resulted in a scattering of people and formation of the nations. In like manner, God has also used migration as a corrective/retributive measure in the lives of people. The book of Revelation, meanwhile, describes the future gathering of the redeemed from the nations formed by migration. Christ's crucifixion makes redemption available to the nations that are products of migration.

There is yet one final dimension of God's revealed use of migration; one that is intertwined with his redemptive plan. He also intended that migration would be instrumental in the making of disciples of the nations. This includes both the movement of God's people to those in need of Christ and the movement of people in need of Christ into close proximity to God's people (as mentioned earlier).

In Romans 10:8–15, the apostle Paul provides an outline of the reverse progression leading to the salvation of any person, whether Jew or Greek. He points out that salvation requires that a person calls upon the Lord. In order to call upon him, the person must believe. Those who believe must hear. Hearing requires a preacher. And this preaching necessitates the sending of a person. The term for sending in verse 15 is *apostellosin*, a derivative of the word from which the title *apostle* comes. The preacher, then, is a sent one. The sending not only indicates a sense of commissioning but also that of movement. In other words, God's plan is to use the movement (migration) of human messengers to communicate the gospel to the nations. Jesus made this clear as he commissioned his followers in Matthew 28:19 to "Go therefore and make disciples of all the nations." Thus, just as migration resulted in the formation of the nations, so too migration is necessary in the reaching of the nations.

As outlined in the book of Acts, this migration, empowered by the Spirit, moved Christian witnesses from Jerusalem, to Judea, Samaria, and to the remotest part of the earth (Acts 1:8). In the words of Stenschke, the book of Acts "shows that—despite and in all tragedy which it involved—these movements of early Christians, be they voluntary or forced, opened

Developing a Theology of Migration

new opportunities for the Gospel."[32] The Acts of the Apostles outlines both the strategic and intentional movements of believers like Paul, Barnabas, and Silas in their missionary journeys (Acts 13–21). It also describes the faithful witness of those who migrated forcibly as a result of persecution (Acts 8:1–4; 11:19–21).

Although the "go" always requires the movement of God's people, God does, at times, use migration to bring those from the nations in closer proximity to the messenger. Those gathered in Acts 2 for Peter's sermon on the day of Pentecost had come from many different areas (Acts 2:7–11). Similarly, the Ethiopian official mentioned in Acts 8 further illustrates how God used migration to bring the hearer near the one sent. This man had traveled a great distance from his homeland in order to worship in Jerusalem. As he journeyed home, he was confused as he read a prophetic Old Testament passage about Jesus. God caused this migrant's path to intersect with that of Philip, who shared the good news about Jesus (Acts 8:26–40).

God, then, not only uses the movement of his followers but also the migration of unbelievers in the evangelization of the nations. As unbelieving people migrate due to family, climactic, economic, or safety factors,[33] they often come into closer proximity to God's people. This was one of the primary thrusts of the apostle Paul in his Mars Hill address (Acts 17:26–28) mentioned earlier. Often, the Father moves people from places of limited Christian access and influence to locations where the good news of Christ can be openly proclaimed. Payne writes:

> we understand that the Lord of the nations is working out his will in the universe, and that the migration of peoples to other lands is not a serendipitous occurrence. Such is particularly true with the migration of the world's least reached people groups to areas of the world where they can freely encounter the gospel of Jesus Christ.[34]

The Creator, then, has designed that migration would play an instrumental part in the discipling the nations. This includes the migration of his people to those in need of his Son. It also incorporates the migration of

---

32. Stenschke, "Migration and Mission," 132.

33. Remigio describes two types of migration: voluntary as people seek "better economic, housing, as well as other social amenities, "and forced migration as people are "expelled by governments during war or other political upheavals." Somewhat overlapping these two categories are the voluntary or forced migrations of refugees fleeing war, famine, or natural disasters. Remigio, "Globalization, Diasporas, Urbanization and Pluralism," 14.

34. Payne, *Strangers Next Door*, 30.

those in need of Christ into closer proximity with those who can proclaim the gospel message.

Summary and Conclusion

The pages of Scripture contain dozens of references to people on the move. In many of these instances, the inspired authors describe these movements as anything but random and much more than a mere human decision. Instead, the hand of God is often clearly depicted as sovereignly and purposefully orchestrating the migration.

Already in the opening chapter of the Bible, it became clear that migration was to play an unmistakable part in the plans of God. From the garden, the descendants of Adam and Eve were to scatter to fill the earth. These journeys would ultimately lead to the formation of the nations and people groups of the world.

The Scriptures also point to God's use of migration as a means of protection of and provision for people. Whether this was movement in the face of famine or opposition, people like Abraham's descendants in the Old Testament as well as the magi and holy family of the New Testament relocated. As they moved, they experienced safety and supply from the caring hands of their Creator.

Additionally, the Bible outlines God's use of migration as a form of punishment and correction. At times, individuals experienced these punitive measures as when Adam and Eve were forced from the garden. But it was also true of larger segments of the descendants of Abraham as both Israel and Judah were forced into exile, migrating from their homeland.

Today, experts in migration often look beyond divine purpose and point to experiential push and pull factors that cause people to move. They describe the movements of people in terms of micro, meso, and macro influences that force or inspire people to relocate internationally. These experts explain migration in terms of theories such as "neoclassical," "dual market," "segmented labor market," and "migration network" theories.[35]

From a human vantage point, most modern migration seems to have one or more human explanations. It is clear why millions from Syria are migrating internally or internationally. They are caught in the crossfires of civil war and are pursuing safety. In like manner, the Wilson Center

---

35. A good, brief summary of these theories is Wickramasinghe and Wimalaratana, "International Migration and Migration Theories."

describes the reasons for the recent migration from Venezuela in these words: "Venezuelans are fleeing a profound economic and political crisis, characterized by the systematic violation of human rights and a deepening humanitarian emergency."[36] One can describe other migrational motives in terms of educational or job opportunities or in the hope of family reunion.

Even though the factors contributing to migration like this may lend themselves to human summarization, the full details of the sovereign plan of God in modern migration defy such simple description. Today's migration is not accompanied by divine, scriptural commentary that offers perfect insight into God's purpose. It is impossible to define all of God's design as he somehow sovereignly reigns.

The apostle Paul described well the difficulty of understanding the purposes of God. In Romans 9–11, he outlines details about complex truths related to the Father's dealings with man through predestination and election. He closes that section with the great doxology:

> Oh, the depth of the riches both of the wisdom and knowledge of God! How unsearchable are His judgments and unfathomable His ways! For who has known the mind of the Lord, or who became his counselor? or who has first given to him that it might be paid back to him again? For from Him and through Him and to Him are all things. To Him *be* the glory forever. Amen. (Rom 11:33–36)

Certainly, modern migration also fits under the category of God's unsearchable judgments and unfathomable ways. One must be careful, then, not to speak for him in imputing divine motives and purposes to twenty-first-century migration in the absence of clear divine revelation.

Is there, however, a principle from this theology of migration that is universally true for each and every movement of people? Is it possible to draw a biblical conclusion about the purpose and intension of God that is true of the Indian student studying in Canada, the Eritrean seeking asylum in England, and the irregular migrant working on a farm in the western United States?

Indeed, there is. In each instance, God desires to use migration to fulfill his redemptive/disciple-making plan. To be sure, there may be divine purpose for the migration beyond this one universal reality. Still, one dare not miss this.

The God who forms the nations has made every provision for their redemption in Christ. Regardless of country of origin or country of

---

36. Van Praag, "Understanding the Venezuelan Refugee Crisis."

destination, God shows no partiality (Acts 10:34–35) but provides equal access to all through the Savior. Regardless of language, the Father welcomes all and, somehow, all will be represented (Rev 5:9) because of the blood of Jesus. Regardless of migration status, regular or otherwise, all have equal standing in the body of Christ (Gal 3:28).

God uses migration as he determines the chronology and geography of man's existence with his redemptive purposes in mind (Acts 17:26–28). He somehow sovereignly orchestrates the times and locations of people so that they might seek him (as the title of this book indicates). The experiences they have and the believers they encounter are strategically intended to create a longing to know him.

With the redemption and discipling of the nations at stake, God's people are also called to migrate. They must be prepared to move. They must go across town to the foreign student, migrant worker, asylum seeker, and international professional that have migrated within their sphere of influence. But they must also migrate across boundaries to reach others who do not yet know the Savior.

3

Defining Ministry to Migrants

As Nasreen arrived on the island of Lesvos, she was . . . well, in modern vernacular, a "hot mess." Fearing for their lives, she had pleaded with her husband to leave behind the sound of bombs, missiles, and gunfire that were commonplace in their hometown in Iran. Saying goodbye to all that was familiar was emotional. They did not know if they would ever see their friends, siblings, and aging parents again. As they tearfully closed the door for the last time on the small convenience store that generated their income, they had no idea what they would do to provide for their future livelihood. To top it all off, uprooting from a culture and language that had become second nature for them was unsettling.

Still, Nasreen felt a temporary wave of relief, as she, her husband, and their two sons arrived in Turkey. They were out of immediate danger, but definitely not yet in their desired destination of Germany. As part of the next step in the journey, they handed an inordinate amount of their life savings to a smuggler. This money was to guarantee passage for them from Turkey's western shore to a nearby Greek island.

Her inner fear resurfaced as she sat in a boat bracing for the next leg of the journey. It was only a short stretch, but over a rough portion of the Mediterranean. To add to the uncertainty, there were fifty others with her in a motor-powered rubber raft designed for a maximum of thirty people and for much calmer waters. After only one of their sons received a life vest, she hung on to her children with a tenacity that hurt their little arms.

That They Might Seek Him

Those in charge of the boat explained to a few of the travelers how to operate the outboard motor. They pointed, as best as they could, to the portion of the Greek island of Lesvos, where they were to go ashore. Finally, the boat launched.

After what seemed like hours, the rhythmic sound of the motor gave way to a sputtering, on-again, off-again revving, before giving way to silence. The eerie sounds of the waves and sea gulls and the boat's predictable rise and fall with each powerful wave multiplied the alarm they felt.

With land seemingly equidistant between points of origin and destination, all eyes turned frantically to the boat's "captain." Surely, with his two minutes of training before departure, he would have the problem solved in seconds. But, no, the motor not only refused to start; it seemed to have nearly detached from the boat, hanging on precariously.

Perhaps it was due to their proximity to the motor or the fact that her husband had proposed a possible solution—whatever the cause, men suddenly pulled knives on Nasreen's family. They threatened the children unless her husband restarted the motor and ensured their safe arrival. While she tearfully did all she could to serve as a human barrier between her children and those threatening, her husband pulled the motor into a more upright position, where it eventually started. But for the next hours of the journey, he burned his arms as he held the hot motor in place, thus ensuring the welfare of their children and guiding all to a safe arrival.

Having landed on Lesvos, the men with knives moved on as if nothing had happened. Unfortunately, moving on did not come so easily for Nasreen. As workers from the United Nations High Commission on Refugees and volunteers from a Christian organization approached her, she could not stop crying. Although they were now one step closer to their desired destination, she was anything but relieved.

How could the UNHCR and those from Samaritan's Purse best help? Yes, she and her family were in desperate need of dry clothes, a hot meal, and housing. They needed people to translate, others to help them with their asylum application. Her kids would need an education. Yes, coming from another faith background, Nasreen and her family needed to learn about Jesus. But there was also the trauma of her experiences that loomed like a fog over all of life.

Defining Ministry to Migrants

How does one best serve Nasreen in her mix of physical, emotional, and spiritual needs? Where does one begin in addressing the daunting temporal and eternal needs?

NOT EVERY MIGRANT STORY is as dramatic as Nasreen's. Nevertheless, every migrant (and every human, for that matter) brings with himself/herself a tangled mix of needs and desires. The Christian workers among migrants have the difficult and at times confusing responsibility and opportunity of sorting through these and identifying which needs are to be addressed and which needs, if any, are to be given priority. What role should the Christian working among migrants play?

These difficult issues are the focus of this chapter. The first portion of this chapter identifies specific biblical teaching for migrant ministry and examples where it is fleshed out. Certainly, these illustrations and instructions help to provide directives for the migrant worker. In the latter half of the chapter, the practical questions of needs prioritization will be explored.

Migration Ministry in the Old Testament

In order to better understand migration ministry in the Old Testament, one must first grasp God's more general missional intentions as outlined in the previous chapter. The Father had a plan for the nations revealed in the "migration mandate" in Genesis 1. Genesis 10 describes some of the resultant nations with their key founders, territories, and languages. God's plan for the nations continued to unfold as he promised Abraham that he would be father to a nation that was to bless other "families" (Gen 12:1–3). Ott provides good insight into the significance of this word: "'Families' comes from the Hebrew term *mishpaha*, which can also mean nation, tribe, or species. This last phrase [of the Abrahamic covenant] is the climax and ultimate intent of the promise. God's blessing on Abraham is not for Abraham alone."[1] The Old Testament reflects God's desire to impact the diverse peoples who had migrated throughout the world as a result of Babel.

As Grisanti states, "It is as God's chosen people that Israel can exercise a mediatorial role with regard to the nations."[2] In many regards, their

1. Ott et al., *Encountering Theology of Mission*, 7.
2. Grisanti, "Israel's Mission to the Nations," 61.

That They Might Seek Him

mediatorial role was passive. Their obedient character and commitment to the law was to attract the surrounding nations to their God (Exod 19:5, 6; Deut 28:10; Isa 49:6). As a result, many have labeled Israel's missional role as a "centripetal mission." Other nations, endeared by God's people, were to move toward the nation and toward God. In so doing, they would experience his blessing and grace. Ott's description is worth noting: "The centripetal movement is that of the nations being attracted as by a magnet to the glory of the Lord manifested in Israel, the nations coming to Zion, and the centralized worship of the Lord in the temple."[3]

To say that Israel was completely passive in the plan of God, however, would be an overstatement. Exceptions to her attractional missional role among the nations are worth noting. Passages such as 1 Chronicles 16:24 and Psalm 96:3 make it clear that Israel was to "Declare his glory among the nations, his marvelous deeds among all peoples." One of the most obvious exceptions to a passive, mediatorial, centripetal mission role for Israel is seen in God's commissioning of Jonah to "arise, go to Nineveh the great city, and cry against it" (Jonah 1:1).

But while Israel's missional responsibility may have been more passive towards nations beyond her borders, she had an active responsibility to those from other nations who lived among them. God was concerned about their interaction with dispersed migrants in their midst. Lines from the Pentateuch clearly instructed his people on how they were to relate to these outsiders. Casey points to three key terms that are used in reference to these non-Israelites:

> There are three Hebrew words that are translated as sojourner/stranger/foreigner/alien and each is used in a general categorical sense, so it depends on which Hebrew word is used because Israel is called to a different relationship with the sojourner depending on a number of criteria associated with each of the three Hebrew words ... Israel is to relate to each category in a slightly different way.[4]

These three Hebrew words are *ger*, *toshab*, and *nakar*.

Ger is found twenty-two times in the Old Testament. New American Standard Bible translators used the words "stranger," "alien," and "sojourner" as English equivalents. The word sometimes refers to an ethnic foreigner who has been circumcised and is now treated as an ethnic Israelite.[5]

---

3. Ott et al., *Encountering Theology of Mission*, 23.
4. Casey, "Caring for the Stranger," 2, 3.
5. Casey, "Caring for the Stranger," 3.

Wright points out that they "were residents in the land, sometimes as members of Israelite households." He goes on to say that "it is sensible to suggest that the noun *ger* should be translated 'immigrant.'"[6]

Using derivatives of the word *ger*, Leviticus 19:34 instructed God's people to love the stranger and alien among them. This was not a command given without foundation or rationale. Instead, they were to love the strangers because God himself loved them and because the Jews also knew from past personal experience what it was to be aliens/immigrants. They thus had a historical, empathetic understanding of being what Wright describes as "economically and socially weak and vulnerable."[7]

Toshab, meanwhile, is used four times in the Old Testament. In the New American Standard Bible, the word is uniformly translated as "sojourner." Based on the contrast of Exodus 12:45 (*toshab*) with Exodus 12:48 (*ger*), Casey points out, "The semantic usage [of *toshab*] most often refers to one with whom Israel is to not relate, especially ceremonially."[8] This is not uniformly the case, as the psalmist refers to himself as a "sojourner" (*toshab*) in Psalm 39:12. And even there, the psalmist is calling out for God to demonstrate his compassionate grace because he is a "sojourner."

Nakar occurs twenty-seven times in the Old Testament. The New American Standard Bible translation of the word varies, including "alien," "foreign," and "strange." Referring often to foreign gods or idols and those who worship them, Israel's response was to be much more distant. Using this word, God gave Moses insight into what would happen after his passing, describing it in these terms:

> And the Lord said to Moses, "Behold, you are about to lie down with your fathers; and this people will arise and play the harlot with the strange [*nakar*] gods of the land, into the midst of which they are going, and will forsake Me and break My covenant which I have made with them." (Deut 31:16)

Once again, Casey makes a key observation:

> In one sense, *nakar* is the category of foreigner to be avoided completely because of their utter opposition to God and immersion in idol worship, but paradoxically, Isaiah especially likes to use *nakar*

---

6. Wright, "Sacred Human Condition," 146.
7. Wright, "Sacred Human Condition," 146.
8. Wright, "Sacred Human Condition," 6.

to draw attention to those outside of Israel, but whom God still pursues until they join themselves to Israel.[9]

Wright echoes those words of caution and compassion by pointing out that the text often speaks of them with a degree of suspicion or antagonism, primarily because they worshiped other gods and so posed a religious threat.

> Nevertheless, Solomon's prayer at the dedication of the temple expressed the surprising assumption that they could be attracted to come and worship the God of Israel in his temple so that Yahweh would answer their prayer, with amazing missional consequences for Yahweh's reputation worldwide (1 Kgs 8:41–43).[10]

Each of these words has its distinctive emphasis and implications. Israel was to relate to each type of person in a different way. Nevertheless, God's ultimate passion is clear. He desired that these people come to him and that his people relate to them. Bosch's conclusion serves as a good summary of Father's heart expressed through his people: "Primarily Israel is to serve the marginal in its midst: the orphan, the widow, the poor, and the stranger. Whenever the people of Israel renew their covenant with Yahweh, they recognize that they are renewing their obligations to the victims of society."[11]

What were the people of Israel to do as they related to these migrants? Christopher Wright summarizes some of the legal rights Israel was to afford to those especially identified as *ger*. These immigrant rights also point to Israelite responsibilities, and they help to give direction to the ministry of those working among migrants today.

1. Protection from general abuse and oppression (Ex. 22:21; Lev. 19:33). The foreigner was not to be mistreated. Christian workers today can be advocates for the rights of immigrants ensuring that others do not take advantage of them.

2. Protection from unfair treatment in court (Deut. 1:16, 17; 24:17, 18). The foreigner was deserving of justice in legal disputes. The Christian worker in the 21st century is able to walk alongside of the immigrant in legal proceedings including visa and residence related issues.

---

9. Wright, "Sacred Human Condition," 8.
10. Wright, Sacred Human Condition," 146, 147.
11. Bosch, *Transforming Mission*, 18.

3. Inclusion in Sabbath rest (Deut. 5:12–14; Ex. 20:8–11). Foreigners were to observe the same patterns of work and rest as their Israelite counterparts.

4. Fair employment practices (Ex. 21:1–11; Deut. 15:12–18). Israelite "employers" were to have labor contracts with foreigners.

5. Prompt payment of wages (Deut. 24:14, 15). Israelites were to pay the foreigner's wages before sunset each day. Each of the last three points depict the need for justice and advocates as present-day Christians employ and/or serve as spokesmen for fair labor practices for migrants.

6. Access to agricultural produce—gleaning rights (Lev. 19:9, 10; Deut. 24:19–22). As foreigners, the Old Testament immigrant was not permitted to own land. They were, thus, given gleaning rights in order to feed themselves. Christian workers today can find appropriate ways to ensure that migrants and refugees have access to food while also ensuring that they assume responsibility.

7. Right to asylum and nonreturn (Deut. 23:15, 16). Those seeking refuge among Israelites were not to be returned. Today's Christian workers can play a key role in ensuring that asylum seekers are protected and that their stories and experiences are properly heard in the asylum process.[12]

Although referenced earlier, the Old Testament instruction to Jews regarding immigrants is perhaps best summarized in Deuteronomy 10:15–19:

> Yet on your fathers did the Lord set His affection to love them, and He chose their descendants after them, *even* you above all peoples, as *it is* this day. So circumcise your heart, and stiffen your neck no longer. For the Lord your God is the God of gods and the Lord of lords, the great, the mighty, and the awesome God who does not show partiality nor take a bribe. He executes justice for the orphan and the widow, and shows His love for the alien by giving him food and clothing. So show your love for the alien, for you were aliens in the land of Egypt.

God had called his people, Israel, then, to a mediatorial missional role among the nations at large and a primarily compassionate, empathetic, justice-oriented missional role among the individual aliens in their midst. Their "ministry" to the outsider was to be one of provision of basic needs and the pursuit of justice on their behalf.

---

12. Wright, "Sacred Human Condition."

That They Might Seek Him

Migration Ministry in the New Testament

The New Testament also echoes God's burning desire to reconcile people from all over the world to himself. In fact, Christ's own purpose statement descriptions of his life helped his listeners to understand the focal point of his earthly ministry. He came for the "lost" and the "many." Luke records him saying, "The Son of Man came to seek and to save that which was lost" (Luke 19:10). Meanwhile, Matthew and Mark summarize Christ's purpose with these words: "the Son of Man did not come to be served, but to serve and to give His life a ransom for many" (Matt 20:28; Mark 10:45).

One may question the Son of Man's global focus, however, if one examines his teaching and ministry only superficially. To the casual reader of the Gospels, the ministry of Jesus and his disciples may seem to have been "particularistic" or exclusively to Jews, to the neglect of the other nations. Jesus did, in fact, define himself as being "sent only to the lost sheep of the house of Israel" (Matt 15:24). In like manner, as he initially commissioned the Twelve for ministry, he instructed them, "Do not go in the way of the Gentiles, and do not enter any city of the Samaritans; but rather go to the lost sheep of the house of Israel" (Matt 10:5–6).[13]

Upon closer examination, however, one discovers Jesus demonstrating compassion for non-Jews and clearly pointing to a coming, focused ministry to the nations as a whole. In Matthew 12, for example, he cited a portion of the Servant Song from Isaiah: "In his name the Gentiles will hope" (Matt 12:21). He healed the Syrophoenician woman, in spite of the "sent only to . . . Israel" statement cited earlier (Matt 15:21–28).[14] He applauded and even rewarded the faith of the Roman centurion in Matthew 8:5–13 by healing the man's son from a distance. He spent time with and offered life to a Samaritan woman at a well (John 4:1–45). In fact, this encounter with her resulted in the faith of many other Samaritans (John 4:41–42). Further, in a region where he was not welcome, Christ's healing of the Gerasene demoniac culminated in Jesus commissioning the man as a witness to his countrymen in the Decapolis (Mark 5:1–20). Further, Jesus illustrated the commandment to "love your neighbor as yourself" with the story of the Good Samaritan (Luke 10:25–37). Through this illustration, Ott et al. conclude, "This commandment [love your neighbor] is given irrespective of

---

13. Tennent refers to passages like these as "particularistic passages." Tennent, *Invitation to World Missions*, 134.

14. Tennent gives greater detail. Tennent, *Invitation to World Missions*, 135, 136.

Defining Ministry to Migrants

the neighbor's religion, social standing, or ethnic background."[15] Additionally, in the Olivet Discourse, he points out the universalistic nature of the mission by saying, "This gospel of the kingdom shall be preached in the whole world as a testimony to all the nations, and then the end will come" (Matt 24:14).

As he looked beyond his own ministry and to that of his followers, Jesus propelled them beyond the geographical boundaries of Israel and the physical descendants of Abraham, Isaac, and Jacob to "all nations" (*panta ta ethne*) in Matthew 28:19. In Luke 24:47, they were sent "into all the world" (*eis ton cosmon apanta*). Mark's gospel makes clear they were to go to "all creation" (*pase te ktisei*) (Mark 16:15). And, in his High Priestly Prayer in John's gospel, Jesus speaks of sending his followers "into the world" (*eis ton cosmon*) (John 17:18). In his final conversation with his disciples prior to his ascension, Jesus pointed to their future worldwide ministry as he promised, "you will receive power when the Holy Spirit has come upon you; and you shall be my witnesses both in Jerusalem, and in all Judea and Samaria, and even to the remotest part of the earth" (Acts 1:8). Thus, not only did the ministry of Jesus have a global focus, but even more so, the New Testament ministry to which he commissioned and empowered his disciples was one to the nations without discrimination.

Ministry as Migrants

As mentioned in chapter 2, this New Testament mission ministry was, first of all, designed to be *ministry as migrants*. This is inherent to the commandment given by Jesus. God's people are to "Go . . . and make disciples of all the nations" (Matt 28:19). The word "go" makes clear that migration is at the core of the mission as God's people move into closer proximity to the nations to reach them. Thus, in contrast to the largely centripetal ministry of Israel, the church's mission is centrifugal and migratory by its very nature. This is depicted in the missionary journeys of the apostle Paul in Acts 13–28 as he used Antioch as the epicenter from which he repeatedly "migrated," taking the gospel to Asia Minor and Europe. It was also at the heart of Paul's drive to go to Spain by way of Rome in Romans 15.

But the migrational "go" of the Great Commission reflects more than just an intentional going whereby a person sets out, like the apostle, with the discipling of the nations in mind. The participial construction can also

---

15. Ott et al., *Encountering Theology of Mission*, 152.

be translated as "while you are going." In other words, missional migration is part of the natural ebb and flow of life. It is for God's people already in motion. It is the commission of all believers, whose movement may be caused by any number of factors. As such, missional migration was also a byproduct of the persecution described in Acts 8:1–4. Because of persecution for their faith, one might expect those early believers migrating to conceal their commitment to Jesus for fear that they might once again be at risk. Instead, these believers saw their migration as an opportunity to proclaim their faith wherever they went. Mission ministry is, then, first of all, ministry as migrants.

Ministry to Migrants

It is, however, often also a *ministry to migrants*. Although easily overlooked, the events recorded in Acts 2 are among the most fruitful examples of migrant ministry. With the Jewish celebration of Pentecost as the backdrop, thousands were gathered in Jerusalem. Many of them had come as pilgrims from other lands. The words of those present found in verses 8–11 point to migrants from a wide radius. On that day, the Spirit of God indwelled and empowered believers to speak in languages unknown to them. The pilgrims responded in surprise:

> And how is it that we each hear *them* in our own language to which we were born? Parthians and Medes and Elamites, and residents of Mesopotamia, Judea and Cappadocia, Pontus and Asia, Phrygia and Pamphylia, Egypt and the districts of Libya around Cyrene, and visitors from Rome, both Jews and proselytes, Cretans and Arabs—we hear them in our *own* tongues speaking of the mighty deeds of God. (Acts 2:8–11)

The linguistic miracle of Pentecost is significant for at least four reasons. First of all, the languages were an external manifestation of the giving of the Spirit, whose coming Joel had promised centuries before and Jesus had prophesied one chapter earlier (Joel 2:28–31; Acts 1:4, 8; Acts 2:4). Secondly, this language event had further prophetic significance as it served to awaken people to the imminent nature of the day of the Lord and the need to call upon him (Acts 2:17–21). Thirdly, this miracle of languages captured the attention of those gathered in Jerusalem. It caused a crowd to gather in curiosity thus preparing people for the message that Peter shared (Acts 2:6–13). Finally, this event made the declaration of the wonders of God even more understandable as people heard of his mighty deeds in their own language (Acts 2:6).[16]

A second example of mission to the migrant from the book of Acts is outlined in chapter 8. Philip had been selected two chapters earlier as one of the seven men who were to serve widows (Acts 6:1–6). Later, in Acts 21:8, he is identified as an evangelist. In the aftermath of the execution of Stephen, Philip engaged in mission as a migrant as he took the gospel to Samaria. Thereafter, an angel directed him and later the Spirit of God prompted him to engage with a migrant from Ethiopia. This nameless eunuch had come to Jerusalem to worship. The man's confusion over and curiosity about a christological passage (Isa 53:7–8) served as the backdrop for Philip's Christ-centered conversation with the man that led to his conversion and baptism (Acts 8:26–38).

This example illustrates another aspect of migrant ministry (although not unique to this type of ministry). There is the need for those who, in sensitivity to the Spirit of God, will come alongside of the migrant in relationship, answer questions, and explain biblical truth. Certainly, it is the Spirit of God that convicts the unbeliever (John 16:8–11). At the same time, he often uses his migrant messenger as an essential part of that conversion equation (Rom 10:14–17).

There is at least one other New Testament passage related to migrant ministry that deserves focused attention. It is in the larger periscope of the Olivet Discourse found in Matthew 24–25 and in the more immediate context of the "Sheep and Goat Judgment" found in 25:31–46. Here is the portion of the passage that is often cited in the context of ministry to migrants:

> Then the King will say to those on His right, "Come, you who are blessed of My Father, inherit the kingdom prepared for you from the foundation of the world. For I was hungry, and you gave Me *something* to eat; I was thirsty, and you gave Me *something* to drink; I was a stranger, and you invited Me in; naked, and you clothed Me; I was sick, and you visited Me; I was in prison, and you came to Me." (Matt 25:34–36)

---

16. It is worth pausing at this point to acknowledge the importance of language in migration ministry. Those engaging in cross-cultural mission often experience challenges when it comes to understanding and being understood. Imagine for a moment that a Canadian Christian goes to Malaysia to work among Rohingya refugees. Challenges like these will be further explored in chapter 6.

That They Might Seek Him

Certainly, the word "stranger" and the kinds of ministries described in this passage parallel the experiences and needs of many migrants. Did Jesus have migrants in mind in his description? Jesus initially identified himself as the one being served. When pressed about how these individuals had served him, he responded, "Truly I say to you, to the extent that you did it to one of these brothers of Mine, *even* the least *of them*, you did it to Me." To serve the "brothers" of Jesus is to serve him.

Who are these brothers? They were, first of all, people with needs as demonstrated by the services rendered to them. Secondly, if the word "brothers" is used consistently with passages like Matthew 12:48–49, these brothers represent Christ followers. Further, if the passage is viewed in light of the Abrahamic covenant and/or dispensationally, "the brothers" could be seen as a reference to the Israelites. After all, God's promise to Abraham and his descendants was that those who bless them would be blessed (Gen 12:1–3). A dispensational interpretation would also place this judgement after the tribulation, a time when the redemptive focus of God turns more pointedly to the Jews. In any case, "the brothers" served were, at a minimum, the needy and marginalized strangers if not more specifically also believers—perhaps even believing Jews during the time of the tribulation.

Still, a commitment to this pericopal, hermeneutical precision dare not turn God's people away from a broader biblical priority. Indeed, serving the marginalized from every ethnicity was central to Old Testament instruction. Similarly, doing good to all people is a New Testament principle (Matt 5:13–16; Gal 6:9, 10) to which believers are called today.

God's intention in both the Old and New Testaments, then, has been to use migration as a means of blessing and reaching the nations. In the Old Testament, the mission of the Jews was largely a centripetal one. Nations were to be attracted to the God of Abraham, Isaac, and Jacob. Meanwhile, those living as migrants among them were to be cared for like other marginalized groups such as widows and orphans. As they reflected on their own experiences as migrants in Egypt, God's people were to ensure justice for the migrants among them. They were also to make responsible provision for them.

In addition to the "come and see" ministry of the Jews, the New Testament mission of the church and of individual Christ followers is largely described as "go and tell." Centrifugal by its very nature, they were to approach mission as migrants—as those on the go to the nations. Still, one also finds examples of mission to migrants. In these instances, God's people were able to represent him while serving others who were residents in a land not their own. Through Christ, then, the *mishpaha* and the *ethnos* of the world are blessed as God's people engage as migrants and with migrants.

Conclusion: Defining Migration Ministry and Priorities in the Twenty-First Century

While the Bible outlines, then, the validity of and even a call to migrant ministry, there remains the question of what this ministry should look like. This chapter along with previous ones have pointed to various aspects of "migration ministry." Still, a clear definition of the nature and goals of migrant ministry is vital for all who engage with it. Ministry to migrants has its share of specific and unique nuances, so such clarification is critical.

Though the focus of mission ministry may seem obvious to any single individual, collectively, church leaders, missionaries, and missiologists have struggled to agree. They have engaged in an ongoing and sometimes polarizing debate over the nature of the mission to which Christ has called his people. The biblical information already explored has seemingly validated helping migrants legally, physically, and spiritually. Should migrant ministry include all of the above? Is it social action or evangelism? Do God's people address temporal needs or eternal ones? Is mission one or the other? Both? One more than the other? Padilla describes the tension well by saying:

> There is general consensus among evangelical Christians all over the world that the church is by nature missionary. But what does that mean? How is the mission of the church defined? What is included in mission? . . . Should mission be identified with evangelism being understood as "the proclamation of the historical, biblical Christ as Saviour and Lord, with a view to persuading people to come to him personally and so be reconciled to God?" Or should mission be equated with social transformation resulting from God's action in history through human agency, which may or may not include the church, as has often been advocated in ecumenical circles?[17]

Others have written extensively on the questions of the nature of mission and on the biblical validity of ministry that engages with the physical needs of people while also addressing spiritual and eternal issues. While some refer to this as "holistic ministry," the term is defined by users in

17. Padilla, "Holistic Mission," 11.

different ways. Christopher Wright, for example, describes mission as building the church, serving society, and caring for creation.[18] For Padilla, meanwhile, mission is a "biblical synthesis" where *holistic* mission "intends to correct a one-sided understanding of mission that majors on either the vertical or the horizontal dimension of mission."[19]

Indeed, Jesus both emphasized and illustrated a two-dimensional, vertical/horizontal ministry to people. He responded to questions about "the great commandment of the Law" (Matt 22:34–40), about the "most important" commandment (Mark 12:28–34), and about requirements for eternal life (Luke 10:25–28) with the same answer. He emphasized love for God (vertical) and love for neighbor (horizontal).

Not only did he underscore both in theory; he also demonstrated both in his ministry practices. A few examples from the Gospel of John serve well here. Christ's commitment to the vertical was evidenced in his invitation to Nicodemus to be born again (John 3:1–15) and his offer to the woman at the well to find in him satisfying water that welled up into eternal life (John 4:1–15). Meanwhile, he demonstrated the value of the horizontal in the feeding of the five thousand (John 6:1–15) and the healing of the blind man (John 9:1–6). In fact, both of the latter miracles serve as good examples of horizontal ministry that gave rise to vertical. The feeding of the five thousand culminated in the Bread of Life Discourse (John 6:25–59). His healing of the blind man resulted in spiritual conversation, clarification, and, ultimately, conversion (John 9:35–41).

Still other New Testament examples could be cited, but perhaps these few suffice. Both love for God and love for neighbor are vital. Spitters and Ellison summarize what is likely accepted by most: "It is a given that missions is not one-dimensional proclamation divorced from demonstration."[20]

Thus, biblical precedent and mandate can be found for both the horizontal and the vertical aspects of missions to migrants. One must ask, however, "Do both have equal value?" Is it, as Padilla has suggested, that majoring on either the vertical or on the horizontal should be avoided?

Missiologists such as David Hesselgrave[21] and Christopher Little[22] argue that the vertical—the proclamation that leads to mature disciples

18. Wright, "Holistic Mission."
19. Padilla, "Holistic Mission," 11.
20. Spitters and Ellison, *When Everything Is Mission*, 44.
21. Hesselgrave, "Redefining Holism."
22. Little, "Case for Prioritism."

Defining Ministry to Migrants

(Matt 28:19, 20; Col 1:28, 29)—should be given priority. Little, in fact, describes the two-dimensional (horizontal/vertical) discussions in terms of two primary camps of *holism* and *prioritism*. Perhaps most defining in his characterization of these two camps is his contrast between the two. In his estimation, holism ascribes the same value to horizontal as to vertical aspects of mission. Little suggests that adherents to holism may criticize prioritism "for being so heavenly minded that it does no earthly good." Meanwhile, in his description of prioritism, Little states, "Evangelism/ disciple making/church planting are more important than other ancillary activities." In other words, for prioritists, the vertical takes precedence over the horizontal. According to Little, proponents of prioritism may see the effort of the holists as "so earthly minded that it does no heavenly good."[23]

Indeed, Jesus underscores the priority of this vertical dimension in his purpose statements for his own coming. As cited earlier, he came to reconcile the *lost* to God and to redeem the *many*. He spoke of the grave misfortune of the individual who "gains the whole world and forfeits his soul" (Matt 16:26). That vertical priority is further outlined in the call of the Great Commission. Matthew describes it in terms of "making disciples" (Matt 28:19). In Mark, the commission is to "preach the gospel" (Mark 16:15). Luke defines the mission in terms of a message of the crucifixion and resurrection of Jesus and repentance that "will be preached in his name to all nations, beginning at Jerusalem" (Luke 24:46–47). Meanwhile, the book of Acts equates the missional assignment with being witnesses of Christ in the power of the Spirit (Acts 1:8).

McGavran argues powerfully for proclamation priority in mission with these words:

> A multitude of excellent enterprises lie around us. So great is the number and so urgent the calls, that Christians can easily lose their way among them, seeing them all equally as mission. But in doing the good, they can fail of the best. In winning the preliminaries, they can lose the main game. They can be treating the troublesome itch, while the patient dies of cholera. The question of priorities cannot be avoided . . .[24]

Thus, without neglecting the very real physical and emotional needs of migrants, those engaging migrants missionally must give priority to their conversion, baptism, spiritual development, and integration into the body

---

23. Little, "Case for Prioritism," 27.
24. McGavran, *Understanding Church Growth*, 24.

of Christ. It is in the local church that both discipleship and diaconal ministry can continue.

But those giving priority to vertical ministry among migrants dare not be guilty of giving a "be warmed and filled" response to the very people they seek to win and disciple. As in Nasreen's story told at the beginning of the chapter, most every migrant arrives in their new host country with a variety of real needs. As Maslow has indicated in his hierarchy of needs, basic physiological and safety needs must often be met before other needs can be addressed. Ministry to the non-spiritual needs of the migrant is important. It must be done with genuine compassion. These acts can prepare the way and establish a foundation for meaningful spiritual ministry. Thus, horizontal ministry opportunities abound. Those serving migrants could offer such things as:

- food help
- housing assistance
- medical help
- trauma/personal counseling
- cultural instruction
- transportation
- educational assistance
- employment assistance
- language help
- legal counsel
- personal visits

In chapter 8, this topic will be revisited in the context of strategy development for migrant ministry. From this chapter, however, it is important to understand that these temporal needs and opportunities must be calculated into a prioritized ministry to migrants. In so doing, migrant lives will be impacted in time and for eternity.

4

Understanding the Political Context

Alejandro is a Spanish mechanical engineer working in an international company. The company produces parts for the auto industry. Even though the parent corporation is headquartered in another European country, company leaders asked him to consider working at one of their major production sites in the United States. Not only did they feel that he has skills to offer the engineering team there, but the company also likes to invest in the growth of their executives by offering them international experience. The contract they presented to him would place him in a facility in a small Ohio town for at least two years, but it could be extended if both Alejandro and his employer agree.

The process of receiving the right work permit and corresponding visa was no small undertaking. The complexity was multiplied by three since Alejandro planned to bring his wife and their small child. Still, they had made good progress, and, it seemed, they were on the verge of approval.

But that was near the end of 2016. Immigration had been a hotly debated political issue in the United States. Diverse opinions had been planks in both the Democratic and Republican candidates' platforms. Even though much of the debate had centered around irregular migration on the southern border, people like Alejandro held their breath not knowing how the next administration would respond to scenarios like his. Would policy change? Would the number of annual international work permits be impacted?

IN RECENT YEARS, TENSIONS over immigration have made headline news in many nations. Controversy over the building of a wall to prevent irregular migrants from entering along the southern border of the United States dominated news cycles for months. Germany felt political and societal backlash as the country allowed two million asylum seekers to enter her land. Meanwhile, the United Kingdom's Brexit exodus from the European Union was rooted, at least in part, in immigration issues related to the freedom of travel of migrants within the EU.

Immigration policy development is both challenging and polarizing. Such policies impact immigrants, citizens, and even partner or neighboring nations. It is no surprise that immigration has garnered media focus, created national political tension, and spawned international controversy. After all, individuals, political parties, national governments, and even church denominations and mission organizations have formulated strong and varied opinions over the types of policies that are appropriate.

This chapter, however, moves beyond the policies themselves as it establishes a foundation for understanding the complexity and the controversy of immigration policy development. Immigration policy is often rooted in one of three different paradigms of international relations. Thus, immigration policies and the corresponding controversies are, in many ways, reflections of an underlying worldview. The three paradigms of international relations differ in their emphasis on the state: its independence, sovereignty, and internal needs and welfare. Concurrently, the paradigms also distinguish themselves in the degree to which they emphasize transnational needs and moral obligations that reach beyond the state.

By understanding these foundational ideas, those with different opinions are better able to understand and appreciate one another. And, when Christian workers among migrants grasp these varied political vantage points, they are better able to work within their ministry context. They are able to appreciate the less visible influences that are swaying political decisions as well as public sentiment.

After exploring these paradigms, this chapter demonstrates how time, events, and media contribute to paradigmatic transitions and tensions. These tensions have placed individuals, political parties, and nations at odds with one another. As a result, Christian workers among migrants may be viewed as appreciated humanitarian workers or as those contributing to an unwanted problem.

Understanding the Political Context

Purpose of Immigration Policy

When discussing immigration policy, people do not typically discuss its counterpart—emigration policy. Most nation-states agree that citizens and legal residents have the right to emigrate. There is widespread endorsement of Amstutz's conclusion: "Because freedom is a basic human right, people are free to leave their homeland"[1] Meanwhile, the right to immigrate is not assumed. When it comes to immigration, the destination country has the right to determine if a migrant will be permitted legal entry and residence. In fact, according to Amstutz, "All nation-states . . . regulate migration. This means that entering a foreign state requires the permission of that receiving country."[2]

Thus, in theory, a person could travel by boat, setting sail freely, without permission, from a shore of a coastal country of their legal residence or citizenship. He/she could sail through the territorial waters reaching twelve miles from shore that still, technically, are part of the nation. This person could continue past the contiguous zone reaching twenty-four miles from shore without the need to apply for authorization. While in international waters, then, the person is subject to a mix of maritime law and the laws of the country under whose flag the boat is sailing. As the person approaches another country, he/she does not, however, have the same freedom to sail through the contiguous zone, into the territorial waters, and to enter another country without proper documentation and corresponding permission from the host country.[3] Of course, it is much more difficult to separate issues of emigration from those of immigration when a person is travelling by land from one nation to its contiguous neighbor. In such instances, one cannot emigrate without immigrating.

Immigration, then, requires the approval of the destination country. Thus, countries regulate immigration through policies that serve two basic purposes. First of all, these policies define the country's intentions for regular immigration. They outline the *who, how many,* and *under what conditions* of migrants being granted entry. Secondly, immigration policies also outline the consequences for violation of the guidelines. These consequences can be directed towards immigrants, employers, or others.

---

1. Amstutz, *Just Immigration*, 16.
2. Amstutz, *Just Immigration*, 16.
3. Law Offices of Charles D. Naylor, "International Waters Laws."

Who, how many, and *under what conditions* are intimately intertwined in policy development. Policies may define desired (or undesired) people in terms of nationality. In some instances, preference is given to people of specific nations with similar cultures, language, and history. Alternatively, some states encourage diversity, allowing entrance to a limited number of individuals from underrepresented nations.[4]

The who of immigration policy may also focus on certain types of employment where the need may be great. Amstutz indicates five preference categories for the US: "persons with extraordinary abilities, professionals with advanced degrees . . . skilled workers . . . special immigrants . . . and entrepreneurs."[5] Meanwhile, unskilled immigrant laborers are, at times, the focal point of controversy over policy development.

Family-based immigration is often another area of concentration in the *who, how many,* and *under what conditions* of immigration policy development. Many nations establish policies allowing for some degree of reunion where a family member is a citizen or legal resident. Priority is typically given to spouses, children, and siblings. Even this seemingly simple aspect of immigration becomes challenging as it can lead to extensive chain migration.

Immigration of refugees and asylum seekers is yet another aspect of migration that is typically regulated by government policy. In the United States, for example, the president establishes a quota of the number of refugees that will be permitted entry each year.[6] Meanwhile, there are those who enter the US asking for protection under asylum status. While the state has no control over the number of those requesting protection, they do have the responsibility of processing the request and determining the outcome.

Immigration policies, then, are first of all designed to establish the parameters for legal immigration. They outline the types and number of people that may be considered for legal entry and residence and under what types of circumstances they may enter. These include such reasons for integration as employment, family reunion, and protection.

Beyond establishing the guidelines for authorized entrance, immigration policies also serve a second purpose. They delineate consequences for the violation of these policies. The state may determine that irregular

---

4. US Citizenship and Immigration Services, "Green Card Through the Diversity Immigrant Visa Program."

5. Amstutz, *Just Immigration*, 25.

6. US Department of State, "About Refugee Admissions."

immigrants, for example, must pay fines or face incarceration or deportation. In many countries, it is considered illegal to employ irregular immigrants. Consequently, employers of these undocumented migrants may pay sanctions for violation of these policies. Meanwhile, smuggling or harboring irregular migrants is also punishable by law in many nations.

Political Paradigms Impacting Migration

If, then, most states agree that policy development is a necessary part of properly regulating immigration, why is it that such tension exists in the policies themselves? Stated simply, not every individual, political party, church, nonprofit organization, or nation has the same convictions about international relations. These varied convictions on migration are rooted in one of three important paradigms of international relations. The paradigms differ in the degree they emphasize state sovereignty and the needs of citizens, on the one hand, or transnational responsibility and the needs of others around the world, on the other. The underlying paradigm embraced by national leaders deeply influences the corresponding state immigration policy.

To begin to understand the paradigms, one can picture a continuum between two extremes. At one end of the continuum is a nation focused on state sovereignty with almost exclusive concern for its citizens. The paradigm represented at this end of the continuum is called *realism*. At the other end of the continuum is a nation focused on transnational/global responsibilities and obligations and the needs of all humankind. The paradigm at this extreme is referred to as *cosmopolitanism*. Between these two extremes is a nation expressing some level of sovereign responsibility for its citizens while demonstrating concern for those outside of its borders. This middle paradigm is known as *communitarianism*. These paradigms are deserving of further explanation.

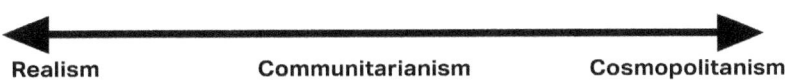

Figure 4.1. Paradigms of International Relations

Realism

Some describe realism in terms of its pessimism about human nature and its concern for the motivations of other nation-states. In the words of Donnelly, "realism's principal purpose is to warn against moralism, progressivism, and similar 'optimistic' orientations. It emphasizes what is unlikely or difficult in international relations, rather than what is worth striving for."[7] Thus, nations embracing realism will tend to focus on their own concerns as they are apprehensive about other nations. Amstutz suggests that realism

> views the world as composed of distinct political communities. Each of these communities is independent and sovereign, and each one pursues its short- and long-term interests in the international system based on its wealth and power. Morality and law are important in how states relate to each other; the obligations of states are chiefly to their own people.[8]

This national self-focus is further illustrated in the words of Korab-Karpowicz, He writes: "Realists consider the principal actors in the international arena to be states, which are concerned with their own security, act in pursuit of their own national interests, and struggle for power."[9]

As is the case with each of these paradigms, realism is more than an overarching, general description of the international relations of a given nation-state as seen over time. It can also represent a pendulum-swing, point-in-time response to an international experience. A nation expressing the realism paradigm will likely focus primarily on its own needs. It may tend to encourage immigration only when a specific niche in the job market cannot be or is not being filled internally. States that reflect this paradigm may pose immigration questions like:

1. How will this type of immigration benefit our country/economy as a destination country?

2. What will this type of immigration cost our country/economy as a destination country?

---

7. Donnelly, *Realism and International Relations*, 194.
8. Amstutz, *Just Immigration*, 80.
9. Korab-Karpowicz, "Political Realism in International Relations."

Communitarianism

On the continuum introduced earlier, communitarianism is located somewhere between an emphasis on citizen-focused state sovereignty at one extreme and global-centric transnational responsibility at the other. States adopting a communitarian approach recognize that there are needs and moral obligations that are beyond those represented in the state. They are less pessimistic about the morals and motives of other nations. Still, the state is the first line of defense in addressing the needs and moral obligations of those within its borders. Once again, according to Amstutz:

> Communitarianism . . . is similar to realism, but it assumes, in addition, that there are transnational interests and transcendent moral values that constrain states. States are the major actors in global society, but morality and law also influence government decisions. According to the communitarian perspective, the international community is a society of states because interstate relations are structured not only by power but also by morality and law.[10]

Communitarian nations attempt to keep both realities in tension as they demonstrate concern for their own citizens and compassion for transnational needs. The immigration implications of the communitarian paradigm are real. Michael Walzer, a renowned communitarian, illustrates the need for some level of restriction in immigration policy inherent to the communitarian paradigm by using the idea of a club and family. A club has an admissions committee that can regulate the qualifications and quota for admitting new members. Similarly, a family feels a sense of concern and obligation—even to family members who are not part of the household.[11]

When it comes to policies of immigration, nations reflecting such an approach may pose the questions:

1. Why are people choosing to emigrate from the states of origin?
2. What should sovereign states of origin do to address the underlying economic or humanitarian issues that may be driving emigration from their state?
3. Is there something our state should do in response to help?
4. To what extent are those wanting to immigrate like us?

---

10. Amstutz, *Just Immigration*, 80, 81.
11. Walzer, *Spheres of Justice*, 35–41.

Cosmopolitanism

Realism, then, is positioned toward one end on a continuum of international relations. A state operating under this paradigm focuses primarily on the welfare of those already within its sovereign control. Communitarianism is a more moderate position that values state sovereignty and sees that as a means of addressing larger global interests and responsibilities. Still, at the other end of the continuum is the cosmopolitan paradigm. This approach to international relations downplays the role of the state even further than communitarians while emphasizing the larger, overarching needs in and moral responsibility to the world. Amstutz offers these insights:

> Cosmopolitanism . . . represents the ideal or just world community where individuals are the primary focus of political action. According to this approach, universal reason provides the basis for pursuing the individual and collective well-being of all humans. Although states exist in the world community, the cosmopolitan approach gives more primacy to global welfare and regards state sovereignty as unimportant."[12]

When it comes to immigration, advocates of the cosmopolitan paradigm typically argue for "global human rights, open borders, and justice rooted in equality."[13] Cosmopolitan nations may not only recognize the desperate economic plight of or the extreme danger faced by people in other countries; they also feel a sense of responsibility. Thus, they may be more generous in granting work visas and in offering refugees asylum, even if within the state employment opportunities are challenged and the tax burden of citizens increases. Those reflecting a cosmopolitan paradigm may ask questions like:

1. What needs and influences are causing people to migrate?
2. What is our responsibility to our fellow man?

Paradigms in Transition

While the perspectives just introduced may describe the international relations of individuals, groups, political parties, or entire countries at any

---

12. Amstutz, *Just Immigration*, 81.
13. Amstutz, *Just Immigration*, 92.

point in time, seldom are people, groups, and nations immoveable in their paradigmatic approach. While the somewhat transient ebb and flow of immigration itself may seem obvious, the sometimes changing perspective of citizens and of the state may be less expected. Circumstances and real-time realities can cause gradual shifts or rapid swings in public sentiment and political policy. Several recent historical realities bear this out.

The fluid nature of the paradigms of international relations is illustrated by two iconic locations in New York City. The first is the Statue of Liberty. Dedicated in 1886, the statue was designed to commemorate the nation's independence declared in 1776 and the freedom of slaves from the abolition movement announced just two decades prior to the dedication.[14] Meanwhile, the statue also came to represent a cosmopolitan invitation to immigrants.[15] In 1903, Emma Lazarus' poem "The New Colossus" was affixed to the statue. Her poem, originally commissioned as a fundraiser for the statue, expresses a welcome to those from other countries needing a fresh start.[16]

> Not like the brazen giant of Greek fame,
> With conquering limbs astride from land to land;
> Here at our sea-washed, sunset gates shall stand
> A mighty woman with a torch, whose flame
> Is the imprisoned lightning, and her name
> Mother of Exiles. From her beacon-hand
> Glows world-wide welcome; her mild eyes command
> The air-bridged harbor that twin cities frame.
> "Keep, ancient lands, your storied pomp!" cries she
> With silent lips. "Give me your tired, your poor,
> Your huddled masses yearning to breathe free,
> The wretched refuse of your teeming shore.
> Send these, the homeless, tempest-tost to me,
> I lift my lamp beside the golden door!"[17]

---

14. National Park Service, "Abolition."

15. National Park Service, "Immigrant's Statue."

16. Arguably, the words of the poem do not accurately portray the sentiment of the day. "Just a year prior to the poem's publication, in 1882, the US Congress had passed the first significant federal law restricting immigration, the Chinese Exclusion Act, which legally forbade Chinese immigrants from entering the United States for more than sixty years." Soerens and Yang, *Welcoming the Stranger*, 46.

17. Lazarus, *New Colossus*.

It is this latter expression of the Statue of Liberty that serves as a symbolic reminder of a more cosmopolitan past of the United States.

Meanwhile, nearly one hundred years later and just two miles away from Lady Liberty, Ground Zero became, for many, the iconic reminder of the need for a different paradigm—one rooted deeper in a perspective leaning in the direction of realism. It was on September 11 of 2001 that the deadliest coordinated terrorist attacks of recent history took place. These attacks took the lives of nearly three thousand people, while more than six thousand were injured. The casualties and injuries were incurred in three locations, including Shanksville, Pennsylvania, the Pentagon in Washington, DC, and the Twin Towers of the World Trade Center in New York City. The latter location, now referred to as Ground Zero, has become the location most widely associated with the day's tragedies. Those terrorist attacks were, by and large, attributed to migrants, albeit regular ones. As a result of those attacks, attitudes towards migrants and migration issues shifted immediately for many. Thus, while Lady Liberty seems to extend a cosmopolitan promise that the nation will "leave the light on for you," Ground Zero betrays, for others, their growing communitarian/realistic mindset calling for increased border control and more restrictive immigration policies.

Such paradigmatic shifts are not unique to the United States. Germany's response to the refugee crisis of 2011–2020 serves as yet another good example. Although Germany had allowed entrance to asylum seekers and guest workers from Turkey and other countries prior to 2000, the public sentiment towards these migrants had been perhaps tolerant at best and antagonistic at worst. But a widespread public attitudinal shift was evidenced in 2011. Beginning in that year and extending beyond, the realities of the danger and destruction of the Syrian Civil War resulted in a wave of migration of more than six million men, women, and children fleeing their country to seek asylum. The resultant desperation captured the heart of Chancellor Angela Merkel and many German citizens. Germany, motivated, at least in part, by the realities of these transnational, global needs,[18] was one of the most generous of receiving countries. Over the following years, the country permitted entrance to nearly two million Syrians and other migrants seeking protection, allowing them to apply for asylum.[19]

---

18. Arguably, Germany's response was not purely out of global concern. The country's long-term need for additional workers and its desire to change its reputation from its Nazi past seem to have also been contributors.

19. These numbers represent a compilation of the annual reports from the Bundesamt fuer Migranten und Fluechtlinge (BAMF).

Moved by media reports and by Chancellor Merkel's confident assurance that "We can do this,"[20] the country seemed to embrace the opportunity and extend a cosmopolitan "herzlich Willkommen" (hearty welcome) to her guests. But by the end of 2015 the pendulum of much public and political sentiment began to swing in the other direction. Citizens recognized the economic challenges, observed only limited short-term integration, and heard reports of acts of terrorism and crime allegedly at the hands of immigrants. The German international public broadcaster Deutsche Welle describes well the attitudinal shift that has taken place more recently: "Germany in 2020 is not the country it was in 2015."[21] Consequently, the cosmopolitan mindset of the middle of the decade has shifted to one of communitarianism and realism.[22]

The transient nature of these paradigms of international relations can be illustrated, then, in different countries, at different times, and for different reasons. Even more recently, COVID-19 realities have had a paradigm-shifting impact that has reached beyond a single country or region. It has impacted migration on a global scale. As the virus spread initially within and around China, other countries continued, albeit cautiously, with somewhat normal international relations and travel—except as they related to that area of the world. With the spread of the virus into more and more nations in every world region, however, most nations pivoted within a few short days to a focus on their own citizens. In March of 2020, in response to the realities of the spreading virus, most nations implemented travel bans that limited who would be permitted into the country and under what conditions. In a blog post just days after these widespread global steps were taken, Hamse Karcic, professor at the University of Sarajevo, described a general global paradigm shift:

> Border closures, quarantines, travel bans and other measures reminiscent of bygone eras of European history played out as the pandemic spread across the continent.
>
> In a bid to contain the public health crisis, the EU decided to close its external borders. Within the EU, Austria, Poland, Hungary and the Czech Republic are reintroducing border controls.

---

20. Through her words "Wir schaffen das!" ("We can do it!"), spoken originally on August 31, 2015, Merkel expressed her confidence that Germany could overcome any obstacles created by the country's admission of refugees by the tens of thousands. Bannas, "Flüchtlingsfrage: Merkel."

21. "Migrants Stuck on EU Doorstep."

22. "Seehofer distanziert sich von Merkels 'Wir schaffen das.'"

What the coronavirus pandemic shows is that realism in international relations is not only alive and well but is back.[23]

The long-term impact of this shift is yet to be seen. Is it temporary? Will it remain limited to COVID concerns? Will it spread into other areas of international relations? It is too early to assess these things conclusively?

As one can see, then, international relations are very sensitive to circumstances and perceptions. The pendulum swing of paradigmatic convictions that impact migration can change drastically and quickly. Realities of desperate needs in another nation can cause public sentiment and political policy to move in the direction of cosmopolitanism. Meanwhile, perceived threats to the economy, cultural identity, and the welfare of its citizens can influence a nation to move in the direction of realism.

Paradigms in Tension

These perspectives of relations are more than paradigms in transition as circumstances and public opinion create an occasional pendulum swing between positions. At any point in time, not everyone within a group, community, or nation shares the same conviction or is transitioning in their thinking at the same rate. These internal paradigmatic differences often create tensions. At the societal level between individuals, in the national arena between groups including political parties, and on the international stage between nations and international communities, diverse opinions on international relations can put people at odds with one another over appropriate immigration policy.

At the individual level, many voice varied views about immigration while, often, not realizing that their opinions are rooted in an underlying paradigmatic conviction. One can picture, for example, a former New York resident who worked in an office building in close proximity to the Twin Towers. At times, the frantic nightmares of the realities of 9/11 are still vivid memories for her. Given her personal experience, it is no surprise that she believes immigration policy must be restricted to protect citizens. In her mind, immigrants must go through an even stricter vetting process. Border control must be tightened. And, as if she needs more reason, the paycheck-to-paycheck realities of her life make it difficult for her to swallow the possibility that her tax dollars are, at least in part, funding the needs

---

23. Karčić, "How Coronavirus Brought Realism Back."

of those entering the US from other countries. All in all, the nation's immigration policies and quotas seem to her to be unreasonably generous.

On the other hand, one can imagine a man who feels a deep sense of moral and spiritual responsibility for the needs of migrants and the plight of asylum seekers. He has watched the media broadcasts that describe and portray the economic perils and safety risks experienced by others. He has heard interviews with migrants entering his country, both regularly and irregularly, in order to feed a starving family or escape a civil war or a drug cartel. As a result, he feels obligated to help. In the face of pressing needs of fellow humans, any position that values limited internal economic discomfort or unfounded concern for national safety more highly may seem to be entirely incomprehensible, untenable, unnecessarily restrictive, and even inhumane. While perhaps unfamiliar with the term, his cosmopolitan concern for humanity is expressed with passion.

These polarizing tensions are more than constructs of theoretical societal strawmen just described. One need only to ask the opinion of others in his/her community to discover individuals with vantage points all across the continuum of paradigms of international relations. And when individuals with differing convictions interact, the conversation can become heated.

Further, these tensions are also played out in a more public, national arena as those with shared opinions band together in advocacy groups or political parties. The 2016 US presidential election is a good case in point. Although immigration had been an important topic in previous elections, it was arguably never so important as in the platforms of the presidential candidates in 2016. James Gimpel, government professor at the University of Maryland, points out, "immigration played an unusually prominent role in the 2016 election, one that issues do not regularly play in presidential contests."[24] Immigration's prominence in the election was, in many ways, initiated by Donald Trump in his 2015 presidential announcement speech. His polarizing description of Mexican immigrants and his promise to "build a great, great wall on our southern border" and "have Mexico pay for that wall"[25] positioned immigration as both a primary and divisive campaign topic. The partisan divide was evidenced in a Gallup poll just four months

24. Gimpel, "*Immigration Policy Opinion*, 1.

25. Trump described immigrants with these words: "When Mexico sends its people, they're not sending their best. They're not sending you. They're not sending you. They're sending people that have lots of problems, and they're bringing those problems with us. They're bringing drugs. They're bringing crime. They're rapists. And some, I assume, are good people." "Donald Trump's Presidential Announcement Speech."

prior to the election. At that point, roughly 60 percent of Republicans and Republican-leaning survey participants favored decreased immigration. In comparison, only 20 percent of Democrats and Democrat-leaning survey participants favored decreased immigration.[26] Thus, tensions between communitarian and cosmopolitan paradigms as they relate to migration were, then, among the issues at the heart of the 2016 presidential election.

Concurrent with these North American realities, immigration tensions rooted in differing paradigms were also brewing in Europe. During that time, many European countries had responded generously to the realities of the refugee crisis by welcoming asylum seekers. Already in place were policies like the Dublin Regulation, which serves to clarify the country responsible for processing asylum requests. Once residence is granted in that country, those migrants possessing a valid residence visa in one EU country had freedom to travel to other European countries allowing them to stay for up to three months.[27] In addition, citizens in an EU country had a largely unrestricted right to seek employment in other EU countries.[28] But while some were welcomed, others entered unknowingly. Consequently, EU leadership in 2015 recognized the need for increased border control. They began to take concrete steps for reducing the number of irregular entries.[29]

But, as the EU leadership focused attention on the refugee crisis and corresponding immigration issues for its member states, the United Kingdom voted in June of 2016 to leave the European Union. This staged Brexit exodus was to take place over the next several years. To be sure, there were many factors that contributed to this decision. Immigration-related concerns, however, were among the key contributors. The research of Goodwin and Milazzo suggests that "increases in the rate of immigration at the local level and sentiments regarding control over immigration were key predictors of the vote for Brexit."[30] Many voters responded to the growing reality of increased numbers of non-UK born people in their communities. By approving Brexit, they expressed their desire to take back control of immigration rather than subjecting themselves to the EU's seemingly generous

---

26. Newport, "In U.S., Support for Decreasing Immigration Holds Steady."
27. European Commission, "Country Responsible for Asylum Application."
28. European Union, "Working Abroad."
29. European Council, "EU Migration Policy."
30. Goodwin and Milazzo, "Taking Back Control?," 450.

guidelines. Thus, cosmopolitan-communitarian paradigmatic tensions were major reasons for the UK's decision to exit the EU.

Paradigms of international relations are, at times, in conflict at the individual level, in the intranational arena, and on the international stage. One final example serves to further illustrate this latter arena. Migrational realities have been a point of concern for the United Nations for some time. According to its own website, "The United Nations came into being in 1945, following the devastation of the Second World War, with one central mission: the maintenance of international peace and security."[31] Thus, the UN's very mission reflects cosmopolitan goals as it speaks to issues of international relations.

It is no surprise, then, that the UN has demonstrated concern for issues of migration. That concern was evidenced shortly after the organization's inception. As a result of World War II, millions of Europeans fled from their homes. In response, the UN formed the office of the United Nations High Commissioner for Refugees.[32] Later, in 1990, the UN adopted the International Convention on the Protection of the Rights of All Migrant Workers and Members of Their Families. Ten years later, they declared December 18 to be an annual International Migrants Day.[33] Further, the UN expressed its migrational concerns in 2016 as 193 member states voted clearly and unanimously to make the International Organization for Migration (IOM) a "related organization" of the UN.[34] The IOM describes its mission as "IOM is committed to the principle that humane and orderly migration benefits migrants and society."[35]

More recently, the UN's interest in migration was demonstrated in its development of the *Global Compact for Migration* in 2018. While acknowledging the sovereignty of individual states, the compact calls member nations to "improving cooperation on international migration."[36] The document further invites this cooperation through twenty-three "Objectives for Safe and Orderly Migration."[37] Although the Global Compact

---

31. United Nations, "What We Do."
32. UN High Commission for Refugees, "History of UNHCR."
33. United Nations, "International Migrants Day: Background."
34. International Organization for Migration, "IOM Becomes a Related Organization."
35. International Organization for Migration, "IOM Mission."
36. Global Compact for Migration, *Global Compact for Safe, Orderly*, 2.
37. Global Compact for Migration, *Global Compact for Safe, Orderly*, 5, 6.

acknowledges individual state sovereignty, the compact advocates for international teamwork in achieving these objectives.

In spite of the fact that the compact is a product of UN collaboration, state endorsement of the compact is completely voluntary. A *BBC News* report indicates, "It's not legally binding and allows countries to remain in charge of their own immigration policy but commits signatories to improving co-operation on international migration."[38] In the end, only 164 of the member nations formally adopted the compact.[39]

But the tensions over the compact's intent and content were not only expressed through dissenting votes. In Brussels, an estimated five thousand people rallied outside of EU headquarters in opposition to the compact. Some held banners that betrayed their frustration with the cosmopolitan leanings of the compact. The banners included statements like "Our people first" and "We have had enough, close the borders." Unfortunately, the rally later turned violent.[40]

Meanwhile, Austrian Chancellor Sebastian Kurz defended the country's unwillingness to sign by pointing out, "We view some points of the migration pact very critically, such as the mixing up of seeking protection with labor migration."[41] Additionally, the United States was one of the earliest opponents to the compact. Ultimately, the US government issued a statement on the UN document pointing out that the US "maintains the sovereign right to facilitate or restrict access to our territory"[42] Thus, paradigmatic tensions related to migration are even felt on the global stage. While many UN representatives created a compact calling for a more cosmopolitan response, individuals and nations responded with a communitarian/realistic reticence to concede their control.

Whether or not a person or group can identify or define any of the three paradigms, it is clear that they are much more than theoretical, academic labels. Every believer, unbeliever, political party, and individual state has his/her/its paradigmatic leanings and convictions (realism, communitarianism, or cosmopolitanism) as they relate to immigration. As a result, tensions between individuals, groups, political parties, and even states can run high.

38. Goodman, "What's the UN Global Compact?"
39. Goodman, "What's the UN Global Compact?"
40. Paris, "Protesters and Police Clash."
41. Murphy, "Austria to Shun Global Migration Pact."
42. US Mission to the United Nations, "National Statement."

Understanding the Political Context

Summary and Ministry Implications

This chapter has begun to explore issues of immigration policy development. While most states embrace a migrant's freedom to emigrate, they recognize that the right to immigrate is in the hands of the country of destination. As a result, countries develop policies that determine *who, how many*, and *under what conditions* immigrants may enter.

Answers to those three critical questions of immigration are rooted in paradigms for international relations. These lines have outlined how three key paradigms impact immigration convictions and policy. *Realism* reflects a certain pessimism about the motives of other nations. Its emphasis on state sovereignty and the welfare of its citizens typically leads to more restrictive immigration policies. At the other end of the spectrum, *cosmopolitanism* emphasizes transnational interests and global responsibility. As a result, cosmopolitans typically rally for the most generous immigration guidelines. *Communitarianism*, meanwhile, is found between these two extremes in its attempt to hold in tension both state sovereignty and global responsibility. Consequently, those embracing this paradigm will generally embrace modest migration quotas and policies.

This chapter has also pointed out the transient nature of national sentiment as it pertains to immigration. Realities like civil war, persecution, and natural disasters abroad can cause the paradigmatic pendulum to swing towards globalism. Meanwhile, internal economic challenges, pandemics, terrorism, and other concerns for national security swing the pendulum towards realism.

As described here, tensions also arise between individuals, advocacy groups, political parties, and nations. Whether the parties involved recognize it or not, the conflict is often rooted in their convictions about the state's commitment to its citizens vis-à-vis its global responsibility. These tensions have led to heated personal conversations, disputes between political parties and candidates, and even demonstrations in opposition to multinational efforts.

For the Christian working among migrants, these are more than mere theories of international relations that explain unimportant policy. These paradigms are more than labels for categorizing positional transitions and describing immigration tensions. By grasping these realities and the challenges inherent to these diverse perspectives, Christians can benefit in a number of ways.

First of all, understanding these paradigms enables Christ followers to critically assess and appreciate the merits of each. Is one paradigm better than another? As will be demonstrated in the next chapter, believers can identify biblical support for all three: realism, communitarianism, and cosmopolitanism. Most Christians working among migrants possess, to some degree, a cosmopolitan concern for global needs. Still, he/she must recognize that the state carries responsibility for its citizens. Consequently, those working with immigrants dare not quickly discard the opinions of those with another perspective.

Secondly, understanding these paradigms enables Christ followers to better understand the dominant attitudes towards migrants in their ministry environment and towards them as workers among migrants. Are citizens warm and welcoming towards migrants—xenophilic? Christian workers may be able to identify historical roots or current events that have led to that cosmopolitan sentiment. This sentiment among the mainstream of the population may engender the engagement of people of different, little, or even no faith backgrounds in addressing the physical and material needs. Christians may, then, discover that the majority of residents in their ministry context respect and appreciate their work.

Alternatively, other believers may serve in areas and countries where the dominant attitudes of citizens towards migrants are those of suspicion and antagonism. This may be rooted in some kind of experience such as acts of terrorism or perception of economic decline. In such situations, believers will often simultaneously identify a more communitarian (or even realistic) emphasis on state sovereignty that is reflected in policy and public opinion. Here, Christian workers may anticipate ill feelings towards migrants—even xenophobia. On the personal level, nationals in the ministry context may not appreciate, or they may even demonstrate opposition to, the work that believers are doing.

Thirdly, understanding these approaches to international relations should serve as a good reminder to believers to look beyond the numbers and the masses in order to see the individual migrant. Indeed, the paradigms are critical and the policies are essential. A nation must answer questions about *who, how many,* and *under what conditions*. In most cases, however, paradigms are reflections of a general mindset. The resultant policies are, then, guidelines designed for nameless people. Ultimately, Christian workers must not lose sight of the fact that these paradigms and policies impact individuals. Even though immigrants travel at times in groups or even caravans, individuals are ultimately in view. They are not numbers or statistics. They are people. Each migrant has his/her story. There is, for each of them, a reason or reasons that brought him/her to the destination country. Just as with other racial issues of the day, believers must guard against stereotyping that only sees a forest and not the individual trees. They must recognize the unique nature of every migrant situation. In like manner, believers can help others to recognize the individual aspect of immigration. By appropriately inviting others into safe and caring encounters with migrants, other mindsets (perhaps even xenophobic ones) can be impacted. Of course, this rationale may seem to be an indirect way of arguing for cosmopolitanism. That is not the intent. Instead of influencing the key *who*, *how many*, and *under what conditions* questions of policy development targeting those who are permitted to enter, this individual recognition is especially for those who have already entered.

Finally, this paradigmatic backdrop also provides a partial foundation for better understanding the role of the believer in policy response and development. Believers have historically engaged with policy development in a variety of ways, from casting a vote for a specific candidate to advocating for policies among lawmakers. What is the appropriate Christian response? How do these paradigms relate to biblical truth? Should Christians passionately advocate for policy development, indiscriminately accept policy handed down, or simply ignore policy as outside of their realm of concern? These are the issues to be examined in the next chapter.

5

Responding to Immigration Policy Development

The church was dying—literally. Their Sunday attendance had dwindled to about thirty-five people. In the previous year alone, the church had said goodbye to three elderly, long-standing members through funerals. Virtually everyone in attendance was over sixty years old.

In addition, no new spiritual life was being infused into the church. Sure, the congregation enjoyed their hymns and were encouraged by some solid sermons. But it had been a long time since they had seen a visitor grace their doors and longer still since someone had come to faith in Jesus as a result of the church's ministry.

But then, one Sunday, a young Iranian asylum seeker came to church. His dark hair stood in contrast to the white heads that surrounded him. His browner skin was different from their Anglo-European tone. Still, his visit was not as random as it may sound. A man in the church had been volunteering at the local community center. The center offered a weekly conversation café for refugees. The man from the church had invested and invited—and the asylum seeker came.

Over the next weeks, this man, Ibrahim, came to faith in Jesus. He was baptized. He started inviting his refugee friends to join him at this little, loving Baptist church. And the church began to reinvent itself. They found new purpose in making eternal investments in those seeking protection in this new country. Over the months that followed, the congregation rallied together and impacted the lives of literally hundreds of refugees. Some of asylum seekers stayed in the area, while others relocated.

But Ibrahim held a special place in the hearts of the congregation. When they learned that his application for asylum status had been rejected and his appeal had been denied, they could not believe it! In their minds, his story of past persecution was convincing. The risks he would face, should he return, seemed to them to be genuinely life threatening. Certainly, his recent conversion to Christianity made the thought of his return to a largely Islamic country even more worrisome. The hearts of those in the church were broken. How could national policy allow for such an obvious injustice?

What should the congregation do in response—not just to Ibrahim's situation, but to all? Should they limit their influence to physical and spiritual ministry? What about political advocacy? With deportation as the next imminent step for Ibrahim, it seemed as if the congregation was without any legal recourse. The state had spoken, and they would have to accept it. But there was for them one further step they could take. It would require great commitment on their part, with no guarantees of a positive outcome, but they were willing. As Quasimodo did with Esmeralda in The Hunchback of Notre Dame, *they would offer Ibrahim "church asylum" or "sanctuary."*

THE LAST CHAPTER IDENTIFIED some of the influences contributing to the development of government policy related to immigration. Paradigms such as realism, communitarianism, and cosmopolitanism often frame policy development. Even those paradigms, however, can change relatively quickly. The realities of a refugee crisis can cause public sentiment and government policy to swing in the direction of cosmopolitanism. The perceived risks of increased criminal activity or acts of terrorism at the hands of immigrants can draw the pendulum towards realism. Independent of any event, the politicization of immigration can influence public opinion and political parties to create polarizing tensions.

This chapter, however, will focus on Christian responsibility as it pertains to political engagement and immigration policy development. How are Christians, churches, and denominations to respond to the political realities in their country and around the world? Should churches and Christians become political advocates for or against policy changes? If so, what should that advocacy look like? In order to respond to these important questions from a Christian vantage point, this chapter will explore the biblical foundation of the paradigms, the limitations of the common frames used to describe migration, and the accuracy of the factual premises of many migration arguments.

Examining the Paradigms

Is one paradigm more Christian or more biblical than another? Just as individuals, groups and political parties, and nations may express an affinity to a particular paradigm, so to with individual believers, churches, denominations, and organizations. It is important here to consider the biblical and practical merits of the paradigms outlined in the previous chapter.

Christian convictions about immigration policy are diverse. Some believers feel an overwhelming compulsion to address the needs of people around the world. For others, nationalism runs high, and it is critical to protect the interests of state citizens. Interestingly enough, the student of the Scriptures discovers biblical support or precedence for all three positions: cosmopolitanism, communitarianism, and realism.

Cosmopolitanism

Many believers naturally resonate with the sometimes desperate needs of all, even those beyond their national boundaries. Amstutz describes it like this:

> When churches and advocacy groups assess migration, they rely not only on moral principles and religious teachings but also on a particular conception of the international community. Such a conception typically corresponds with cosmopolitan norms rather than with communitarian precepts.[1]

The cosmopolitan paradigm resonates with a Christian worldview in its emphasis on the inherent value of all people. Christians understand that Adam and Eve and, consequently, all of humanity were created in the image of God (Gen 1:27; Jas 3:9). All people, regardless of nationality, have intrinsic value because they reflect the likeness of their Creator. In the words of Daniel Carroll, "The creation of all persons in the image of God must be

---

1. Amstutz, *Just Immigration*, 96.

the most basic conviction for Christians as they approach the challenges of immigration today."[2]

This cosmopolitan value of all people is expressed in corresponding concern for all people. Christians are to share this concern, independent of a person's background. Regardless of national origin or cultural history, believers are invited to demonstrate compassionate love for the neighbor in need. The Parable of the Good Samaritan illustrates that sense of obligation. Jesus' story applauds the man who, in spite of the cultural differences, demonstrated compassion and love for his "neighbor" (Luke 10:25–37).

Amstutz expands beyond this and points to further extrapolations from this shared value of and concern for all people. He writes:

> A Christian worldview shares with cosmopolitanism three central beliefs: first, the well-being of persons is primary; second, because people are entitled to dignity and equality, the international community is an inclusive moral society; and third, because the international community is a coherent ethical society, people have a right to migrate.[3]

One dare not overlook this last concept of an international community. This is at the very core of Christian identity. Although believers may point to affiliation with a specific local church, they are, at the same time, part of the universal church or body of Christ (1 Cor 12:13). In that regard, Christians from Africa share much in common with their European brothers and sisters. But this global concern is not only for believers in other parts of the world. It is also for those who have not yet by faith embraced Jesus Christ (Matt 28:19). Independent of their specific location, then, Christians possess a sense of international identity and responsibility.

Because of their shared conviction of universal human dignity, Amstutz points out that many Christians trend towards a cosmopolitan viewpoint. This, then, results in a sense of moral responsibility and global solidarity. Consequently, immigrants have freedom of movement from their origin country to a host country.[4] Whether that broader sense of ethical society of humankind grants the right of immigration, however, is not as obvious from Scripture. Still, because of this shared biblical foundation, many individual Christians, churches, denominations, and organizations

---

2. Carroll R., *Bible and Borders*, 13.
3. Amstutz, *Just Immigration*, 97.
4. Amstutz, *Just Immigration*, 97–99.

have embraced such a cosmopolitan perspective and advocate for generous and flexible immigration policies.

Communitarianism/Realism

Rather than global solidarity, communitarianism and realism emphasize communal identity. Amstutz summarizes the position by saying, "[Communitarianism] views the world as a society of nation-states in which the primary responsibility of such states is to protect and enhance the rights and well-being of its own people while also caring for all people."[5] Thus, the primary focus is on citizens within a geopolitical region. It is on those residing legally within the boundaries and under the political influence of the state. Many of these individuals share a common history, language, ethnic background, and cultural expressions. Adherents to this paradigm believe that an individual has the right to emigrate from their country of origin, but the right to immigrate is granted by the host country.

Once again, there are elements of this paradigm that resonate with biblical teaching. Indeed, the state does possess both the right and the responsibility to develop and enforce laws and policies that benefit and protect its citizens. In fact, the earliest evidences of and instruction for human government within the Bible are ones granting the responsibility for protective punishment. Even before God gave the Old Testament Law to Moses, he instructed Noah after the flood with these words: "from *every* man, from every man's brother I will require the life of man. Whoever sheds man's blood, by man his blood shall be shed, for in the image of God He made man" (Gen 9:5b–6). Thus, the very image bearing emphasized by Christian cosmopolitans is an essential aspect of realism's responsibility of the state to protect and punish. Similarly, in the New Testament, Paul also reminds believers of this responsibility of the state. He points out that governing authorities are from God (Rom 13:1). In fact, he instructed believers in Rome that the governing authority in their day was "a minister of God to you for good" (Rom 13:4).

When it comes to policy development, believers must develop a rounded view of Old Testament instruction given to the Jews. As seen in chapter 3, God gave the nation of Israel clear instruction regarding the "alien" and "sojourner." But there are also biblical examples of a more extreme, protective realistic paradigm. This is illustrated after the time of the

---

5. Amstutz, *Just Immigration*, 13.

exodus at the time of the conquest. As God's people migrated from bondage in Egypt, they returned to the land promised them hundreds of years before. This land was inhabited by immigrant people from other nations. These people embraced false religions, and many practiced idol worship. Rather than, in a cosmopolitan manner, allowing his people and these nations to live together in close proximity, God desired to protect his people from these nations and their religions. His protective desire was so strong, in fact, that he called his people to drive such people from their midst and and/or to annihilate them (Deut 7:1–6). Of course, the point here is not that immigrants should be banished or destroyed. Instead, it is that there is biblical precedent for the restriction of residence of immigrants—precedent that parallels modern realism and communitarianism.

Given the complexity of the issues and the biblical support for or anecdotal evidence of realism, communitarianism, and cosmopolitanism, one must recognize that all have their place. In fact, Amstutz takes the argument one step further. He states, "If Christians are to contribute to a more effective and more just immigration policy, the analysis and advocacy of immigration reform must also incorporate communitarian precepts that acknowledge the fragmented nature of global society and the essential role of states in advancing human rights."[6]

Other Guiding Biblical Principles

One can identify, then, scriptural examples and/or instructions pointing toward the various paradigms of international relationships. Beyond the arguments for a specific paradigm, there are also other important biblical principles that should be considered. These, too, help believers in the formulation of convictions, establishment of expectations, and engagement with and response to policy development. Here is a sampling of additional principles that believers must factor into their engagement.

1. Believers must have realistic expectations of policies, policy makers, and immigrants. All of humanity possesses not only equal value but also, as a result of the fall in the garden of Eden, equal depravity (Rom 3:23). This depravity spans all of the nations as "both Jews and Greeks are all under sin" (Rom 3:9). But the realities of human sin are much broader than willful acts of disobedience, and they reach beyond

---

6. Amstutz, *Just Immigration*, 99.

biblical doctrines of anthropology and soteriology. They also impact immigration and policy development. Because of humankind's sinful propensity in a fallen world, policy developers will, at times, make decisions that seem self-serving, lack a rounded perspective, and/or fail to reflect perfect knowledge. The challenges of immigration policy development in a fallen world evade simple solutions. Amstutz describes the evasive nature of finding immigration policy answers in the 1940s and 1950s with these words: "Ironically, the efforts to expand border regulation spawned increased illegal immigration."[7] And the challenge is not only with policy development. Depravity is also inherent to the immigrant. Not every potential immigrant possesses noble purposes as he/she seeks to immigrate or after immigration. There is, thus, a need for vetting and protective policies. In short, because of the reality of the fall, immigration and corresponding policy development will never be perfect in this age.

2. Christ followers must carefully differentiate between Israel and the church. Although the church is comprised of both Jew and Gentile (Eph 2), Jews also have a distinct future promised in the Old Testament that is yet to be fulfilled (Rom 9–11). God's plan for the sanctification of his people in the New Testament was neither expulsive nor destructive in the same way that it was with the Israelites at the time of conquest. Instead, his plan for the sanctification of his missional disciples acknowledged that they lived in a sinful world, that they were not of this world, and that they were sent into this world as divine ambassadors (John 17:13–19). Their missional sanctification, then, was achieved through their commitment to the Word of God. One must be cautious, then, in applying to the New Testament church Old Testament teaching and promises intended for the people of Israel. Are there Old Testament principles that apply? To be sure. Still, one must exercise exegetical discernment.

3. When it comes to immigration, Christians must learn to differentiate between the church and the state. This statement is an extension of the second point above. Israel was both a spiritual entity and a nation. In that regard, it was a theocracy. The laws of God were also the laws of the state. Most nations today make neither claims nor pretenses of being a theocracy—at least not a nation attempting to exclusively

---

7. Amstutz, *Just Immigration*, 10.

use biblical principles and moral standards as the substance of its law. Because of the Great Commission and the Great Commandment, the church possesses, by its very nature, a global interest. The state, meanwhile, has a regional focus. Amstutz writes, "Because the kingdom of Christ is a universal community, the church can exist without boundaries. The state, however, is responsible to control the affairs within its territorial boundaries."[8] Of course, Christians can encourage the adoption of laws and policies that reflect biblical values. To be a Christ follower is to be one who will live in a tension between a sense of global obligation and regional responsibility.

4. Jesus followers who work among refugees must recognize their dual citizenship in two different kingdoms. On the one hand, they are citizens of the state with corresponding rights and responsibilities. At the same time, they are citizens of a heavenly kingdom. It is in this future, heavenly kingdom that ultimate justice and the union of people from every tribe, tongue, people, and nation (Rev 5:9) will be realized. Immigration is a much broader issue than the *who, how many*, and *under what conditions* questions that immigration policies in the current kingdom seek to answer. Broader issues of economic, sociological, climactic, and ethnic inequalities that often contribute to issues of migration will only be perfectly addressed in Christ's future kingdom. This heavenly kingdom and its King are yet to come (Matt 6:10; Phil 3:20; Rev 20:1–6).

Critiquing the Frames

In addition to the paradigms that provide a foundation for immigration policy perspective, there are also word pictures that are used to describe immigration. In his article "Interrogating the Legal/Illegal Frame: Trump Administration Immigration Policy and the Christian Response," Matthew Shadle describes these frames as a means of understanding immigration. He defines frames as "mental images or shorthand—people use to make sense of the immigration issue."[9] Specifically, he points to cosmopolitan descriptors such as "land of immigration" and "melting pot." He mentions more restrictive, comparative word pictures where the state is compared to

---

8. Amstutz, *Just Immigration*, 104.
9. Shadle, "Interrogating the Legal/Illegal Frame," 91.

an *organism* or *home*. Even the use of contrasting terms such as *legal/illegal* provide a framework through which migration is viewed.[10]

While these words or migrational frames may be helpful, they also have their limitations. Issues of immigration are more complex than any single frame can easily portray mentioned. No one of them tells the full story. In fact, any one of the frames can introduce an aspect of migration that not only oversimplifies the issues but also influences people to a policy perspective based on that limited aspect. Describing a country, for example, as a "land of immigrants" may be an accurate portrayal of the origin of past generations. Still, it may fail to address the historic reasons for generous immigration practices. In like manner, it may assume that there is good reason for perpetuating these historical practices into the future.

In 1908, Israel Zangwill introduced a Broadway play by the name *The Melting Pot*.[11] That frame has served as a common immigration descriptor of nations and their approach to immigration for more than a century. Since then, the term has been used to convey an expectation that immigrants eventually drop their cultural and national identity. The result is that the receiving country is not as consciously impacted by the presence of immigrants.[12] The long-standing use of this frame can create presuppositions and expectations. This can lead to a critical assessment as citizens encounter immigrants whose language skills and level of acculturation are out of sync with nationals who grew up in the culture and with the language as their mother tongue.

Organism is a frame that, on the one hand, conveys the living nature of a state. When it comes to immigration, however, the term can be used to describe a delicate living entity that must be protected from viruses and infections outside. Indeed, the state has the responsibility of determining who is permitted to enter its borders. Still, the idea of protecting from infection sensationalizes the risks of immigration. It encourages a heightened level of suspicion of immigrants.

Because *home* is an experience common to all, it is, on the one hand, a familiar frame. Individuals know what it is to invite and welcome family members, friends, and acquaintances into their house. On the other hand, most individuals are reluctant to allow strangers into their homes. This frame can be used to cast doubt on the immigration vetting process that a

---

10. Shadle, "Interrogating the Legal/Illegal Frame," 91.
11. Zangwill, *Melting Pot*.
12. Orosco, *Toppling the Melting Pot*, 13.

country has in place. Has the state explored the immigrant's story and past adequately, that they can be invited into the "home" and permitted to stay?

To be sure, use of the frame *legal/illegal* provides an accurate description of a person's status in a host country. For some, however, it also communicates a moral good/bad character assessment.[13] Even more, the terms do not always tell the full story as they fail to explore the person's experiences in their country of origin and reasons for immigration. While this background information does not change the immigrant's legal/illegal status, such an understanding can impact the corresponding moral judgment. In an attempt to neutralize the character assessment often inherent to the terms, many choose to use the words *regular/irregular*.

Thus, frames can serve a useful purpose in providing word pictures or shorthand for understanding immigration. In determining the nature and direction of their political engagement, Christians must recognize the frames' ability to subtly sway public opinion. Although such frames can be helpful and even accurate, they are often incomplete. Immigration is complex with many facets that defy the ability to summarize with a single word picture often rooted in a particular paradigmatic preference.

Analyzing the Arguments

In assessing appropriate political engagement and immigration policy development, believers must also sort through passionate statements from zealous individuals, political parties, and media sources. While these statements may, at times, seem convincing, fact-checking such statements is essential. In some ways, the politicization and media coverage of migration have painted a black-and-white picture of the issues. At times, the exaggeration of specific concerns has oversimplified complex issues or inaccurately portrayed reality. Following are concerns that are often raised.

"*Migrants take jobs from citizens.*" To be sure, there have been, are, and will be instances, isolated or widespread, when that argument accurately reflects the realities within a host country. Still, the argument has two important underlying assumptions. First, the argument assumes that the number of people needing employment in the host country exceeds the limited number of employment opportunities. Secondly, this argument is only valid if the citizens would accept and fulfill the responsibilities of

---

13. It is not surprising that many use less volatile terms like *regular/irregular* in describing immigrant status.

the position if offered. Even though this complaint is often raised, these underlying assumptions are not always accurate.

In some host countries, the number of jobs exceeds the number of employable adults. Eurostat, the statistical office of the European Union, projects that the German population, for example, will decline in the decades to come due to low birth rates.[14] LeBor points out that, in the face of this population downturn, "the German economic machine needs new workers."[15] Larson describes the broader situation of the entire continent with these sobering words: "The reality is that Europe is demographically dying and desperately needs immigrants to survive."[16] Part of this "survival" is reflected in monetary realities. For some countries, the population growth rate is inadequate to keep up with employment needs. For countries facing a future marked by more jobs than potential employees, migrants can offer strength to a diminishing workforce. Where that is true, immigrant employees are not necessarily taking jobs from citizens.

The second assumption rooted in the complaint that "migrants take jobs from citizens" is that non-migrant citizens would willingly accept the specific employment position and fulfill its responsibilities. In the United States, for example, a 2014 Pew research survey indicated the following types of job where immigrants were disproportionally represented.

- personal appearance industry (nails, hair, and skin care)
- construction industry
- agricultural industry
- textile industry
- maids and housekeeping
- transportation industry (taxi and chauffer)
- media and communication[17]

Why is it that so many migrants fill jobs in these areas? Certainly, there is no single answer. The strong representation of migrants in specific types of employment at times illustrates the fact that they are often the most qualified and have earned a reputation for doing the work with

14. Eurostat, "Population Projections."
15. LeBor, "Angela Merkel," 14.
16. Larson, "Current Trends in Islam," 88.
17. Blanco, "Immigrant Workers Are Most Likely."

excellence.[18] In some instances, however, migrants are willing to do work that others are not. Agricultural work, for example, can be difficult work in extreme conditions. Not every national is willing to do such work. This is not always a statement about the type of work. It can also be wage related. Some migrants are willing to do the work at a wage that citizens will not.

"*Migrants cause a financial drain on the economy.*" In order to properly respond to this statement, one must recognize the many variables involved. The assessment may change according to the type of migrant, the type of visa, or the migrational generation in focus.

An asylum seeker or refugee, for example, may enter the country initially as one who is dependent on the state for the provision of essential needs. While this person contributes to state and local needs through purchases, he/she may not be making a significant contribution to the state through tax dollars paid on earnings. In the US, for example, asylum seekers must wait a minimum of 150 days from the time of applying for asylum before they can apply for authorization to work.[19] Refugees, meanwhile, having been vetted, may work upon arrival in the US.[20] They may also, however, be the recipient of public benefits independent of their employment status.

Regular migrants with corresponding dependents, meanwhile, could be in the host country with a temporary work visa, student visa, or permanent residence permit (green card). Each of those statuses affords the holder certain employment opportunities and social benefits. Thus, there are many variables that determine whether a given migrant is receiving more from the state than he/she is contributing.

Finally, irregular migrants have no legal right to work, but also very limited access to social benefits. In most situations, these benefits include limited emergency medical help, educational opportunities for children, and other nutritional assistance.[21] The reality is, however, that many do work. Some of them are paid "under the table" without taxes withdrawn. Others, in spite of their irregular status, voluntarily pay taxes in the hopes

---

18. "Just How Vital Are Immigrants?"
19. US Citizenship and Immigration Services, "Asylum."
20. US Citizenship and Immigration Services, "Refugees."
21. National Conference of State Legislatures, "Federal Benefit Eligibility for Unauthorized Immigrants."

that their payments will someday reflect favorably on them as they pursue their documentation.[22]

Each of those factors leads to potentially different responses to the concern of financial drain created by migration. Still, bottom line, what do the numbers say? Blau and Mackie report the following based on US immigration research:

> For the 2011–2013 period, the net cost to state and local budgets of first-generation adults (including those generated by their dependent children) is, on average, about $1,600 each. In contrast, second and third–plus generation adults (again, with the costs of their dependents rolled in) create a net positive of about $1,700 and $1,300 each, respectively, to state and local budgets. These estimates imply that the total annual fiscal impact of first-generation adults and their dependents, averaged across 2011–13, is a cost of $57.4 billion, while second and third-plus generation adults create a benefit of $30.5 billion and $223.8 billion, respectively. By the second generation, descendants of immigrants are a net positive for the states as a whole, in large part because they have fewer children on average than do first generation adults and contribute more in tax revenues than they cost in terms of program expenditures.[23]

"Migrants increase crime rates and raise the risk of terrorism." Certainly, there is anecdotal evidence that seems to validate that concern. There are migrants who have, indeed, been guilty of crime and they have been among those performing acts of terrorism. The events of 9/11 in the United States have already been referenced. More recently, on New Year's Eve 2015–16, more than 1,250 sexual assaults were reported in twelve different cities in Germany. Reportedly among the perpetrators were migrants and asylum seekers. Indeed, there are instances when migrants have committed crime and have been guilty of acts of terrorism.

Can one, however, say that the risks increase with more migrants? Are migrants more likely to commit crime? Of course, it must be noted that irregular migrants are guilty of the crime of either crossing the border without proper documentation or of overstaying their visa. Are there also other crimes of which they are guilty at a higher rate than nationals?

Based on an assessment of 2014 US census data, the CATO Institute would say no—at least not in the United States. As they examined the

---

22. Hallman, "How Do Undocumented Immigrants Pay Federal Taxes?"
23. Blau et al., *Economic and Fiscal Consequences of Immigration*, 12.

data on incarceration of adults eighteen to fifty-four years old in the US, they concluded:

> There were an estimated 2,007,502 natives, 122,939 illegal immigrants, and 63,994 legal immigrants incarcerated in 2014. The incarceration rate was 1.53 percent for natives, 0.85 percent for illegal immigrants, and 0.47 percent for legal immigrants . . . Illegal immigrants are 44 percent less likely to be incarcerated than natives. Legal immigrants are 69 percent less likely to be incarcerated than natives.[24]

One must keep in mind that migrants face the risk of deportation if convicted of a crime. That is undoubtedly a strong deterrent to criminal activity. Even irregular migrants run the risk of drawing attention to their undocumented status if they are investigated for suspicion of committing a crime.

What about terrorism? Although focused once again on the United States, the CATO Institute has produced some helpful research on acts of terrorism over a period of time from 1975 to 2017. They conclude that: "Including those murdered in the terrorist attacks of September 11, 2001 (9/11), the chance of a person perishing in a terrorist attack on U.S. soil committed by a foreigner over the 43-year period studied here is 1 in 3.8 million per year."[25]

Indeed, over that forty-three-year period, one does see a greater occurrence of acts of terrorism committed in America by foreign-born perpetrators. In response, appropriate preventative steps must be taken. At the same time, the best of policy development will not totally eliminate the risk. While border controls and proper vetting procedures are essential, not every foreign terrorist entered the country with terrorism in mind. Some, much like local citizens who become terrorists, convert to radical groups later as legal residents of the country.

"*Migrants disturb cultural homogeneity.*" It is difficult to fully assess this concern. What is meant by "cultural homogeneity"? How is that measured? These questions of integration are examined in greater detail in chapter 6. Still, this statement is deserving of a brief answer in this context.

For many, language skills are the quintessential reflection of cultural homogeneity. Their expectation is that migrants should be proficient in

---

24. Landgrave and Nowrasteh, "Criminal Immigrants."
25. Nowrasteh, "Terrorists by Immigration Status."

the mother tongue of their new destination country. Still, the reality is that many first-generation migrants have limited language abilities.[26]

Immigration not only often creates a mix of languages. It can also create religious diversity that is, at times, objectionable. As Germany experienced its influx of immigrants during the refugee crisis of the 2010s, many of them brought faith orientations with them that were different from the Catholic and Protestant expressions familiar to the Germans. Local Germans feared the possibility of mosques dotting the landscape, of calls to prayer sounding through the community, and of animals being sacrificed as part of their worship. Such diverse faith expressions introduced by immigrants can create strong emotions. Thus, people like immigrant and seminary professor Dr. Markus Zehnder suggest that migrants and especially refugees should be directed toward host countries where the immigrant shares the dominant faith expression.[27]

While cultural homogeneity may be desired by many, others appreciate heterogeneity. Rather than a "melting pot" frame of uniformity, they enjoy a "salad bowl" frame of diversity. They intentionally visit "China Town," where they shop. "Little Italy" is listed as one of the city's many attractions. Many intentionally choose the "mom-and-pop" authentic Mexican restaurant over the chain version. Ethnic and cultural diversity is, in that regard, valued by many—including some of the very ones advocating for cultural homogeneity.

In short, the common complaints about immigration, often rooted in differing paradigms of international relations and frames of understanding, are not always as clear-cut as they seem on the surface. Before embracing them at face value, one does well to dig deeper to explore related realities. Then, one is better equipped to respond to the corresponding implications for policy development.

Developing a Christian Response

To this point, this chapter has outlined some of the biblical foundations of and corresponding strengths and weaknesses associated with paradigms

---

26. In a 2007 report, Hakimzadeh and Cohn indicated that 23 percent of first-generation migrants in the US were fluent. Meanwhile, the statistics jump to 88 percent and 94 percent respectively for second and further generations. Hakimzadeh and Cohn, "English Usage among Hispanics."

27. Zehnder, "Bible and Immigration."

of international relations. It has pointed out the some of the shortcomings of oft-used frames and statements used to describe, express concerns about, and influence public opinion regarding immigration. How, then, does a Christian, a church, or a denomination respond to this politically charged topic?

Commit to Consistent Prayer

History has demonstrated that the resolution of immigration challenges is beyond the best efforts of state governments and even of international coalitions. Prayerful supplication directed to the all-powerful, all-wise God of the universe is humankind's best recourse. He "is able to do far more abundantly beyond all that we ask or think" (Eph 3:20). It is not only on the situation or in the people prayed for that the resultant impact can be seen. As Henri Nouwen stated, prayer also impacts the one praying. He writes, "Prayer challenges us to be fully aware of the world in which we live and to present it with all its needs and pains to God."[28]

Specifically, one can pray for divine intervention. Through God's action, what seems impossible can become reality (Eph 3:20). In the Old Testament, seas were parted (Exod 14), a city collapsed (Josh 6), the sun stood still (Josh 10), rain was withheld and returned (1 Kgs 17, 18), and men escaped fire unscathed (Dan 3). In the New Testament, people were healed (Matt 8:5–13), prison doors were opened (Acts 12:6–19), and storms were calmed (Mark 4:35–41) all at the request of people. Praying for a movement of God in humanly impossible circumstances is key.

Additionally, one can pray for human wisdom. God offered to grant Solomon anything he might ask for as he began to lead the nation of Israel as king. He applauded Solomon's request for wisdom (1 Kgs 3:1–15). In the New Testament believers are invited to pray for wisdom. Wisdom is something that God gladly gives (Jas 1:5–8). Certainly, wisdom in the face of the multifaceted issues of immigration is essential.

Believers should pray for governing authorities in potential host countries as they develop policies (1 Tim 2:1–7). They can pray that God guides the leaders in having an appropriate concern both for citizens and for potential immigrants. Through prayer, they can invite God's wisdom as key leaders determine the best response to irregular migrants. One dare

---

28. McNeill et al., *Compassion*, 114.

not underestimate the value of prayer for government leaders. After all, it is God who can direct the heart of kings (Prov 21:1).

In a similar manner, prayer for countries of origin is also critical. As has been described earlier, migration is not just the product of factors pulling people to a new location. There are also push factors. Thus, many emigrate from apparent poverty to perceived abundance, from persecution to perceived safety, from stifling limitations to perceived opportunity. Prayer for emigration countries and their corresponding leaders invites God to intervene by providing solutions and by granting wisdom to those leading the country.

Prayer for the actual immigrants is also important. Many of them face pressures of language learning, acculturation, and integration. In addition, some have experienced great trauma. Accomplishing the simplest of tasks can seem overwhelming in their new environment. Prayer invites God to help them as they adapt.

Offer Extensive Education

Beyond consistent prayer, believers also carry the responsibility of providing extensive education in this important facet of contemporary life. This education is in the context of the discipling role that Christ has given to his church (Matt 28:18–20). Soerens writes, "Perhaps the greatest need in terms of education is having Christians develop a biblical worldview on immigration."[29]

Such a biblical worldview sees through contemporary sensationalism. It enables believers to recognize both the merits and the flaws of positions and reports from media and political leaders. Done properly, this worldview will incorporate both global concern and government responsibility, thus enabling believers to understand and appropriately struggle with the biblical tensions illustrated in the paradigms of international relationships.

This need for education is demonstrated in a 2015 survey conducted by Lifeway Research. Lifeway invited responses from one thousand US evangelicals on contemporary immigration issues. When asked about the top influences of thinking on immigration, only 12 percent of evangelicals indicated the Bible. This was the fourth most influential contributor to

---

29. Soerens and Yang, *Welcoming the Stranger*, 209.

evangelical thinking behind their own interaction with immigrants, with friends and family, and with media.[30]

But the church's educational responsibility extends beyond the church and reaches into the public arena. Amstutz suggests four essential ingredients for the creation of educational documents that are shared publicly. First of all, rather than finding select verses to support a policy preference, "such studies will include a competent and comprehensive overview of biblical teachings relevant to the particular issue being addressed." Secondly, these documents should acknowledge their presuppositions regarding church and state as they "highlight the political theology used in applying Scripture to the specific temporal political and social problems." Thirdly, the teachings should reflect an understanding of the complexity the issues as they "show a sophisticated knowledge of the issue being examined." And, finally, "an effective teaching document must provide a sophisticated integration of faith and politics" that examines possible responses and anticipated results.[31] Educational documents such as these can serve the church's role in the public arena as described by Martin Luther King Jr. King: "The church must be reminded that it is not the master or the servant of the state, but rather the conscience of the state."[32]

Consider Appropriate Advocacy

Political positions are represented on a spectrum between a generally pro-immigration, cosmopolitan global emphasis and a more restrictive, state-sovereignty emphasis aligning more with the realism paradigm for international relations. In like manner, Christian thinking is also positioned along this same spectrum. Some evangelical leaders tend to side with a more cosmopolitan vantage point, like Soerens and Yang, who define immigrant advocacy as "amplifying the voices of those who are marginalized, standing in the gap to present the realities of injustice around the world to those in positions of influence who can help change the situation."[33] Many Christian advocates understand the church's role in the terms mentioned earlier as being "the conscience of the state."[34]

30. Lifeway Research, *Evangelical Views on Immigration*, 16.
31. Amstutz, *Just Immigration*, 233–35.
32. King Jr., "A Knock at Midnight."
33. Soerens and Yang, *Welcoming the Stranger*, 210.
34. King, Jr., "Knock at Midnight."

For some, advocacy for immigration policies is rooted in God's passion for the marginalized. It is compassionate concern for the orphan, the widow, and the alien (Exod 22:21–24; Deut 10:18, 19; Jas 1:27). It is doing what Proverbs 31:8–9 expresses: "Open your mouth for the mute, For the rights of all the unfortunate. Open your mouth, judge righteously, And defend the rights of the afflicted and needy." For them, advocacy takes the form of moving beyond educating fellow believers to influencing policy makers towards the creation of more generous immigration policies. Those like Soerens and Yang encourage believers to engage in advocacy by engaging with elected officials and demonstrating church support for generous immigration policies,[35] increased and accelerated family reunion, and amnesty for qualifying irregular migrants.

Other Christian leaders, meanwhile, place their emphasis on the recognition of state sovereignty. They identify weaknesses in the more generous mainstream of Christian advocacy for immigration. Amstutz, for example, argues:

> Their advocacy has been informed by a one-sided ethical assessment that has given precedence to compassion and inclusion and has de-emphasized justice and the rule of law . . . church reports have generally neglected important subjects such as citizenship, the rule of law, and the legitimacy of immigration rules.[36]

Instead, Amstutz encourages a more principle-based teaching that emphasizes the educational role of the church mentioned earlier. This education provides biblical principles that should guide thinking through the tangled web of sometimes competing issues and interests. According to Amstutz,

> As decision-makers continue to weigh the merits of how best to strengthen the American immigration system, Evangelical groups can make a unique contribution to the policy debate by illuminating biblical norms, identifying key ethical issues, and showing how proximate justice can be advanced.[37]

Although it may be a less direct form of political advocacy, this teaching can, nevertheless, influence the thinking of policy makers.

---

35. Soerens and Yang, *Welcoming the Stranger*, 211–13.
36. Amstutz, *Just Immigration*, 216.
37. Amstutz, *Just Immigration*, 189.

Responding to Immigration Policy Development

Believers, then, must carefully consider their biblical response to policy development. Soerens expresses his support of policy-oriented advocacy for immigration reform by saying, "Engaging politically means we have to move away from the false dichotomy of the secular versus sacred. God's dominion is over everything, including government, and we are called to push back the darkness in every corner of our society."[38] Meanwhile, Amstutz encourages believers to recognize the very reality that Soerens dismisses. He writes,

> The central dilemma in applying Christian norms to immigration issues is how to illuminate the distinctive responsibilities in the City of God and the City of Man . . . Due to sin, the pursuit of justice and the common good is a never-ending task. Scripture does not provide specific guidance on how to reconcile the competing—at times conflicting—demands of spiritual and temporal authority. Instead, believers must follow Jesus' admonition: "Render to Caesar the things that are Caesar's, and to God the things that are God's" (Matt 22:21).[39]

Thus, believers must carefully examine these issues when it comes to immigration advocacy. What does the Bible teach? Is it an approach of direct advocacy through political engagement driving towards a specific policy? Or is it one of indirect advocacy through moral education helping policy makers to think biblically? To what extent should it be promotion of a specific policy? To what extent should it be presentation of biblical principles that others are encouraged to embrace as they formulate policy?

Finally, one dare not forget that immigrant advocacy is more than just a broadscale attempt to impact policy development for immigrants as a whole. Advocacy can also be expressed on a personal level as believers walk alongside individual immigrants, ensuring that their voice is heard and that the migrant understands the voices of others. Christians can play an important role in ensuring that immigrants understand what documents to complete and how to complete them. Believers can be a great asset as they provide transportation to legal/visa appointments. And, in some instances and in isolated countries, "church asylum" or "sanctuary," as expressed in the opening story, can be a form of advocacy to prevent deportation while authorities are invited to review the asylum seeker's case once again.[40]

---

38. Soerens and Yang, *Welcoming the Stranger*, 179.

39. Amstutz, *Just Immigration*, 217.

40. Ökumenische Bundesarbeitsgemeinschaft, "Welcome."

6

Taking Steps Toward Contextualization and Integration

Together with his family, Ismail has lived in Birmingham, England for more than twenty years. Although he has a permanent residence permit allowing him to stay in the country, he has no desire to become a citizen. Among other things, citizenship would require an English proficiency at the B1 level, which is well beyond his current limited facility in the language—in spite of his longevity in the country.

Ismail has a large circle of people with whom he has regular contact. Their story is similar to his. They, too, are Iranians who immigrated in search of better, more stable job opportunities. They share his mother tongue of Farsi. In fact, his social needs seem to be more than satisfied through this network of relationship. They meet regularly for meals and to play pasur, a card game, in the winter or bocce ball in the summer.

Although now retired, even his employment had not forced him outside of those relationships or into a strong need for learning English. His employer had hired many migrants like him. They were willing to do some of the work that many Brits were not—and at a wage that Brits scoffed at. His boss, fluent in English and Farsi, has served as a translator and mediator for him and the other Iranian employees. In some ways, Ismail hardly feels as if he lives outside of his homeland.

When Ismail receives English mail, including government information and requests, he relies on his sons for help. These two young men essentially

Taking Steps Toward Contextualization and Integration

grew up in Birmingham. They are fluent in both languages and adept in both cultures. They are able to translate the important documents and tell their father how to navigate the system in order to care for any requests.

Behind closed doors, Ismail's neighbors express frustration. To them, Ismail seems friendly enough with a ready smile and "hello," but the conversations cannot go further without great effort to communicate even the simplest of ideas. They find it difficult to understand why a man who has been in the UK so long is still unable to communicate better in English. To add to their frustration, the music coming from his flat is too loud. Or maybe it isn't the volume that annoys them. Perhaps it is just the fact that the genre, words, and beat, though muffled, seem so foreign to them. And then there is the strong smell of unfamiliar cooking spices that emanates from his apartment into the rest of the complex. Because all of this seems so different to his neighbors, they choose to demonstrate cordiality while keeping their distance.

In spite of their Islamic background, Ismail and his family claim faith in Jesus. They came to Christ early in their time in the UK through contact with a Christian-based community center that offered help to migrants like them. Unfortunately, they have struggled to find a place of belonging in a British local church. Years ago, they did attend a Farsi-speaking congregation. As their children grew into adolescence, however, they resisted attending. The children were identifying more and more with the British culture than the culture of their parents' homeland. The boys did not want to be further segregated and identified even more as foreigners by associating with the church. In the meantime, the leader of the Farsi-speaking fellowship had moved, interest waned, and the church closed.

THE CHALLENGES OF THE otherness of both the migrant and the native born are real. These differences find their most observable expression in language, culture, and religion. Indeed, Jesus followers with a missional heart should readily engage the "foreignness" of their ministry. They must be bold enough to engage relationships with migrants, transcend language challenges, appreciate aspects of cultural differences, enjoy the music and food, and understand the religion of the nation's guest. This is the vital but challenging process of ministry contextualization. Christ followers and migrants are blessed when contextualization is part of the ministry.

Still, the migrant may remain on the fringe, failing to integrate and be integrated. Migrant integration may be likened to the proverbial middle school dance. The music is playing while boys stand on one side of the gym and girls on the other. In this case, the potential dance partners are the migrants on one side and the state, the neighborhood/community, or even the local body of Christ on the other. Although one can point an accusing finger at the migrants for not "dancing," the dance of integration is not as one-sided as many imagine. Just as there are responsibilities represented on both sides of the gym, so too integration is not only defined by migrant initiative. In their *Home Office Indicators of Integration*, Ndofor-Tah et al. describe the mutual responsibility like this: "Integration is multi-directional—involving adjustments by everyone in society. Integration depends on everyone taking responsibility for their own contribution including newcomers, receiving communities and government at all levels."[1] Nations, communities, churches, and individuals are richer when steps toward integration are taken.

Contextualization and integration are the two themes for this chapter. The events of Babel in Genesis 11 introduce the backdrop for the present-day issues related to both. These implications are outlined in the first section. The next section addresses the unique difficulties of contextualization faced in migrant ministry. Finally, the chapter closes by addressing broader issues of integration on the national, societal, and ecclesiological level.

Understanding Babel

The events of Babel can be understood in terms of roots and fruits. The fruits of the God's decisive action flow from the causal roots of humankind's sin and his eternal plan. They had rebelled against God's clear command to "fill" (Gen 1:28; 9:1) or "populate" (Gen 9:7) by congregating (Gen 11:4c), rather than migrating. In pride, they desired to make a name for themselves (Gen 11:4) rather than acknowledge the glory of their Creator and Judge. Idolatry was likely also a part of their building as they sought to build a tower that would "reach into heaven" (Gen 11:4).

The fruits of the events of Babel, meanwhile, are manifold. In response to God's decisive action out of his desire that the earth be filled, people

---

1. Ndofor-Tah et al., *Home Office Indicators of Integration*, 11.

Taking Steps Toward Contextualization and Integration

moved away from Babel as the epicenter. Genesis 10 depicts this post-Babel migration. In that chapter, one finds four recurring words with repercussions that are still felt today: "territories," "clans," "nations," and "languages." As people migrated, they initially traveled as families to new locations, to which they acclimated. People groups with unique linguistic and cultural expressions were the outcome.

Still today, the roots and fruits of Babel represent great challenges to the Great Commission enterprise of the church. Men, women, and children without Christ are naturally prone to the same kind of sinful roots of rebellion, pride, and idolatry. Every Christian seeking to make disciples of the nations experiences the realities of what began on the plain in the land of Shinar and spread over the face of all the earth. The differences in language, culture, and religion present the need for contextualization.[2] Thus, the need for contextualization of the methods and message is universal to every attempt to make disciples of the nations.

Contextualization in Migrant Ministry

But, while every mission effort faces the need for some level of contextualization, there are some unique facets of the fruit of Babel that impact migration and migration ministry today. What is it that makes contextualization in migrant ministry different from contextualization in other ministry contexts?

Migrant Ministry is Multilayered

First of all, it is often multilayered. In some instances, the Christ followers may themselves be immigrants who have relocated to the destination country. They, then, are seeking to contextualize ministry in order to be as fruitful as possible within a culture and language that may not be their own. They are themselves working through the challenging process of enculturation. Certainly, this offers a point of resonance with other immigrants. They

---

2. The incarnation of Jesus (John 1:14) is an amazing example of contextualization. Further, the apostle Paul clearly expresses his commitment to contextualization in 1 Corinthians 9:19–23. The depth of his commitment to contextualization is illustrated as one contrasts his sensitivity to the background of a Jewish audience in Psidian Antioch (Acts 13:16–41) with his approach to those on Mars Hill in Athens (Acts 17:22–31). For further elaboration, see Flemming, *Contextualization in the New Testament*, 65, 75.

bring a special sensitivity—even empathy—to the table as they interact with others. Even if they come from a culture and language different from that of the immigrant, they share with migrants the common experience of trying to do the very thing they are doing or have done—live in a country that is not their home.

Beyond that, and even for those serving in their own country of origin, the multilayered aspects of contextualization are illustrated in the fact that migrants in a given region may come from any number of cultural backgrounds. Thus, at any point of time, Christ followers may be working with multiple cultures. At times, this will not only be on an individual basis. It could be in a group context, where an unpredictable mix of Asians, Africans, Europeans, North Americans, South Americans, or Oceanians may be present. Within the group, then, cultural values and expressions may be vastly different. This diversity may find its expression in such things as methods of communication (direct/indirect), perspectives on time orientation (monochronic/polychronic), and reactions to transgression (guilt/innocence, fear/power, shame/honor).

Migrant Ministry Represents a Moving Target

Yet another challenge that sets contextualization in migrant ministry apart from many other types of mission is the fact that it is often a moving target. If a Christ follower works among Somalis in Somalia itself, he/she is on their turf. Somalis there are immersed in their own culture, language, and faith—all of which remain fairly constant. Working with Somalis in Columbus, Ohio is quite different. They bring with them their culture, language, and faith and can choose to isolate themselves in a Somali enclave in their new country. Still, they are now immersed in a larger societal context that is vastly different. The influences and pressures inviting them to completely, or even incrementally, adjust their cultural, religious, and linguistic perspectives and expressions are real. Each Somali may respond differently. Some may more tenaciously embrace their grip on their former identity. Others may loosen it and allow themselves to embrace the differences they experience in their new culture.

As a result, the same kind of contextualization that connects with Somalis in Somalia may not work with Somalis in Columbus. Likewise, the contextualization necessary for Somali ministry in Columbus last month may not be as useful next month. In that regard, there may be no monolithic description of those being reached. Contextualization in migrant ministry can be a moving target.

Other authors have addressed topics of contextualization amidst cultural differences. Rather than outlining this good content, some of the source material is mentioned. In his book *God's Image and Global Cultures*, Kenneth Nehrbass addresses some of the current cultural realities from God's perspective.[3] Storti's *Figuring Foreigners Out* offers practical insights that invite the reader to engage with personal and cultural comparisons.[4] Christ followers can utilize Rokeach's Value Survey for better understanding key goals and behaviors of other cultures. Georges outlines the need for contextualization according to how a culture processes life: guilt/innocence, shame/honor, and fear/power cultures.[5] The reader does well to consult the works of these authors and others such as Hall[6] and Lingenfelter.[7] All the while, one must keep in mind that contextualization in a migrant ministry setting can be a multilayered moving target.

Integration in Migrant Ministry

The language, cultural, and religious differences originating in Babel[8] also create integrational challenges. For many, it is difficult to feel at home amongst people who think, act, talk, and worship differently. The challenges are bidirectional. Migrants find it hard to mix with others while those from the host culture feel uncertain about, threatened by, or even fearful of the guests. And these integrational struggles are felt in relationship with the state, community, and church.

National, societal, and ecclesiological: these are the three different facets of migrant integration outlined in the remainder chapter. It is difficult to disentangle these three from each other, and it is important that the servant of God understands the far-reaching implications of each. On the state level, paradigms of national integration are reflected in policy development

---

3. Nehrbass, *God's Image and Global Cultures*.
4. Storti, *Figuring Foreigners Out*.
5. Georges and Baker, *Ministering in Honor-Shame Cultures*.
6. Hall, *Silent Language*.
7. Lingenfelter and Mayers, *Ministering Cross-Culturally*.
8. If one traces the rebellion of man to its origin, one could also argue that these differences were a result of the fall in Genesis 3 or even of the cultural/migration mandate of Genesis 1.

and expectations for integration are expressed in citizenship requirements. By grasping these, Christ followers are better equipped to understand the overall government sentiment and help immigrants in a journey that always includes residence and sometimes involves naturalization. At the societal level, the two directional nature of integration exposes concrete indicators of integration. When those ministering among migrants appreciate these, they are able to point internationals toward the establishment of bonds, bridges, and links that serve as relational connections. Finally, by examining the ecclesiological dimensions of integration, followers of Jesus explore different approaches to immigrant inclusion at the local church level. They are, then, better positioned to strategically and prayerfully consider appropriate church models for the specific ministry context.

National Integration

Immigration policy and citizenship requirements are tangible and visible expressions of values that run much deeper. These values are, in part, illustrated by the three major paradigms of international relations outlined in previous chapters: realism, communitarianism, and cosmopolitanism. The state's underlying leaning will be played out in procedures that outline which people will have opportunity to integrate into the destination country, under what conditions, and in what numbers. National integration, then, begins with the policies that determine the *who* and the *how many* questions of immigration.

From the state perspective, what does it, then, mean for a migrant to integrate once he/she has immigrated and is resident in a new country? The state's requirements for citizenship are good indicators of its integration goals for migration. Most countries reflect one or a blend of four theoretical citizenship models: imperial, folk, republican, or multicultural.

According to the imperial model, each citizen is placed under the same leader(s). Although scarcely visible today, the only requirement for imperial citizenship was subordination to the leaders and laws of the state. This subordination outweighed any expectations related to language acquisition, cultural adaptation, or historical knowledge.[9]

The folk model excludes immigrant minorities from citizenship. In other words, a person must share the language, lineage, and culture of the

---

9. Haas et al., *Age of Migration*, 89.

Taking Steps Toward Contextualization and Integration

state in order to be a citizen. Some African and East Asian countries reflect this model.[10]

Countries like the United States, meanwhile, serve as examples of nations utilizing a republican model of citizenship. According to this model, immigrants and minority groups are able to become citizens if they adhere to the laws and adopt the culture of the state.[11] In the United States, the specific requirements include English skills and historical and civic awareness, in addition to minimum prior legal residence and moral character.[12]

Finally, the multicultural model of citizenship includes the expectation of submission to national laws. It differs from the republican model, however, in that it allows for immigrants and minorities to more thoroughly preserve their cultural/ethnic distinctiveness.[13] In recent decades, countries like Canada and the Netherlands have reflected elements of this model at times.

Of course, not every immigrant becomes a citizen. Some are given the status of "legal permanent resident." In the US, for example, these immigrants are also known as "green card holders." They have the right to unrestricted (but legal) employment, to own property, to receive financial assistance for higher education, and to serve in the military."[14] Still others are afforded the option of dual citizenship.[15]

In summary, a nation plays a key role in determining which people are able to integrate and what the expectations of integration are. These are rooted in corresponding paradigms of international relations and models of citizenship. By understanding these, the Christ follower seeking to reach immigrants can:

- better understand the general public sentiment about immigrants;
- assist/encourage the migrant in the legal process;

---

10. Haas et al., *Age of Migration*, 89.
11. Haas et al., *Age of Migration*, 89.
12. US Citizenship and Immigration Services, "Citizenship and Naturalization."
13. Haas et al., *Age of Migration*, 89.
14. US Department of Homeland Security, "Lawful Permanent Residents."also known as "green card" holders, are non-citizens who are lawfully authorized to live permanently within the United States. LPRs may accept an offer of employment without special restrictions, own property, receive financial assistance at public colleges and universities, and join the Armed Forces. They also may apply to become U.S. citizens if they meet certain eligibility requirements."
15. Haas et al., *Age of Migration*, 90.

- identify potential ministry opportunities in helping immigrants move toward such citizenship essentials as language and cultural acquisition as well as historical and civic awareness.

Societal Integration

Beyond national integration, there is also the challenge of societal integration. Regardless of the degree of diversity desired or permitted within a country—independent of the extent to which a state emphasizes its sovereign rights or expresses concern for those on the move—migrants not only reside in a country but they must also function in a society. They do well to integrate and to be integrated in their local community.

Defining societal integration is no simple undertaking. Certainly, the opinions and expectations of the other citizens within the host country are varied. Although there is no single, agreed-upon definition of societal integration, the description outlined by the UK's Home Office[16] paints a good picture of successful integration: "This is what true integration looks like—communities where people, whatever their background, live, work, learn and socialise together, based on shared rights, responsibilities and opportunities."[17] In other words, integration is experienced as people graciously engage one another in the neighborhood, schools, and places of employment. It is reflected in joint learning and in social interaction.

If defining societal integration is not simple, assessing it is even more difficult. It is not like measuring the qualifications for naturalization, where the migrant's cognitive awareness of a nation's history or its political process is quantified through a standardized test. It is often more complex than the migrant's ability to effectively communicate in a specific language or even understand cultural norms.

But, while there is indeed an intangible facet to societal integration, that does not mean that it is totally void of indicators. Once again, academicians and practitioners in the UK have developed some of the most helpful tools in this area. Although specifically intended for their societal context, the principles are transferable to other migrant societies that share

---

16. The UK's Home Office is responsible for keeping citizens safe and the country secure. It "is the lead government department for immigration and passports, drugs policy, crime, fire, counter-terrorism and police." UK Home Office, "About Us."

17. Ndofor-Tah et al., *Home Office Indicators of Integration Framework 2019*, 10.

Taking Steps Toward Contextualization and Integration

the same integration objectives. The next several paragraphs will attempt to summarize the helpful ideas from their framework. They will also serve to outline possible points of connection and assistance for those engaging migrants for the sake of the gospel.

The UK Home Office utilizes four primary headings with fourteen different domains that serve as indicators of integration. Markers and Means "represent the context in which integration can take place as well as major areas of attainment that are widely recognized as critical to the integration process."[18] Social Connections "recognize the importance of relationships to our understanding of the integration process and elaborate different kinds of relationships that contribute to integration."[19] Facilitators "represent key facilitating factors for the process of integration."[20] The Foundation "represents the basis upon which mutual expectations and obligations which support the process of integration are established."[21] The headings and domains of these indicators are depicted in table 6.1.

Markers and Means	Work	Housing	Education	Health & Social Care	Leisure
Social Connections		Bonds	Bridges	Links	
Facilitators	Language & Communications	Culture	Digital Skills	Safety	Stability
Foundations			Rights & Responsibilities		

Table 6.1. Indicators of Integration Framework[22]

For Christ followers working among refugees, these domains may seem far removed from their call to make disciples among the nations. They must keep in mind, however, that societal integration has a bearing

18. Ndofor-Tah et al., *Home Office Indicators of Integration Framework 2019*, 16.
19. Ndofor-Tah et al., *Home Office Indicators of Integration Framework 2019*, 16.
20. Ndofor-Tah et al., *Home Office Indicators of Integration Framework 2019*, 17.
21. Ndofor-Tah et al., *Home Office Indicators of Integration Framework 2019*, 18.
22. Ndofor-Tah et al., "Home Office Indicators of Integration Framework 2019," Ndofor-Tah et al., *Home Office Indicators of Integration Framework 2019*, 15.

on the long-term well-being of the migrant. Successful societal integration will, in many ways, play a key role in the migrant's longevity in the country, his/her ability to function independently, and the degree to which others include or marginalize the migrant.

Without compromising his/her priority of making disciples, each of these should be of concern to the Christian working among migrants. At the same time, many of these domains represent potential onramps for interaction that can also open the door for meaningful ministry. Here are brief statements outlining principles and opportunities for migrant workers as they relate to each of the fourteen domains.

1. Rights and responsibilities: The migrant worker can serve as an advocate for justice and humane treatment of migrants.

2. Language and communication: Those engaging migrants missionally can use language learning in classes, conversation settings, and one-on-one instruction as a means of helping them integrate and of gospel presentation.

3. Culture: Here again, Jesus followers can use formal and informal culture instruction as a means of helping migrants to learn the norms and expectations within the receiving country.

4. Digital skills: Although the next chapter describes a general technological literacy among migrants, by offering classes or personal instruction on computer and Internet usage, the believer helps the migrant connect with resources and become more independent.

5. Safety: Ministry among migrants must be a safe place where those serving have been properly vetted. Workers should also recognize that immigrants will be guarded in communication until they know that listeners can be trusted.

6. Stability: Believers can come alongside migrants in helping to bring encouragement that levels off some of the roller coaster ride of unpredictable highs and lows.

7. Bonds: Followers of Jesus can recognize that they are often a part of a relational network that includes others like them.

8. Bridges: Servants of Christ can connect people to resources, organizations, and services while exercising caution in not creating unhealthy dependence or exclusivity.

Taking Steps Toward Contextualization and Integration

9. Links: By connecting migrants to the right organizations and resources, Jesus followers play an important part in the integration process.
10. Work: When a Christian worker among migrants helps with things like language, digital skills, resume development, interviewing skills, and specific job skills training, they are positioning the migrants to provide for themselves, to develop other relationships, and, often, to earn favor with others from the culture.
11. Housing: Christians can serve migrants by offering or directing them towards good housing options.
12. Education: Once again, by offering help in the form of things like language and digital learning environments, Christians help to equip migrants for other educational options.
13. Health and social care: Believers can assist with the health and mental welfare of migrants by being sensitive listeners and by providing clinics, counseling, or transportation to such services.
14. Leisure: Travel, sports, and recreational opportunities are meaningful avenues for ministry and integration.

These fourteen domains represent onramps for connection, ministry, and societal integration. The Christ follower, however, must keep two cautions in mind. First, by engaging with any or all of these meaningful/necessary domains, he/she dare not lose sight of gospel priority. As outlined in chapter 3, believers cannot allow the priority of discipleship to be completely drowned out by the cry of the urgent. Secondly, believers should recognize that societal integration (and really all types of integration) is not fully dependent on their efforts. While they can provide the right kinds of opportunities in the rights domain, there are still the initiative of the migrant and the response of others in the community. Certainly, Christians can encourage both, but they cannot control either.

Ecclesiological Integration

Incorporation into the church is yet another aspect of integration, to which those making disciples among migrants should give attention. Of course, inclusion in the universal church is something facilitated by the Spirit of God as he places all believers into the singular body of Christ (1 Cor 12:13). This facet of ecclesiological integration, then, is within the less visible church.

There is, however, still the very practical question and challenge of integration into the more visible, local church in the community within the receiving country. Certainly, in eternity, a great multitude "from every nation and *all* tribes and peoples and tongues" will gather around the throne to worship. But, what about now? Will they be gathered together in individual, local bodies of Christ? Is it possible and desirable to integrate people from diverse backgrounds, cultures, languages, and nationalities into a multiethnic church? Or, is it more prudent to establish monoethnic churches where those from the same cultural context grow in faith? One discovers biblical examples of both as outlined in the following lines. Although there is no single right answer to the question of mono- or multiethnic churches, there are some important thoughts to keep in mind in making a strategic decision.

Integration into Multiethnic[23] Churches

From the biblical record, one observes that the first church was birthed out of diversity. The church in Jerusalem, though possibly described as monoethnic in terms of the Jewish roots of its members, was comprised of a varied group of Jews. Padilla states:

> On the day of Pentecost, the gospel was proclaimed to a large multitude of pilgrims that had come to Jerusalem for the great Jewish Feast of the Weeks (Acts 2:1–13). The heterogeneous nature of the multitude is stressed in the narrative by reference to the variety of languages (vv. 6–8) and lands and cultures (vv. 9–11) represented among them.[24]

Prill adds that this church arose initially from a diverse linguistic milieu (2:5–11) and later reflected a strong contingency of Jews from both Hebrew and Hellenistic backgrounds (Acts 6:1–7). He further argues that the church in Antioch (Acts 11:19–30), the leadership team in Antioch (Acts 13:1, 2), the missionary teams for the second missionary journey

---

23. While the author recognizes that there are nuances of differences in meaning between the words *cultural* and *ethnic*, the corresponding literature uses both terms and does not always make a distinction between them. For this reason, in the following discussion both terms are used interchangeably.

24. Padilla, "Unity of the Church."

(15:40—16:3), as well as the churches established (Acts 16—18) reflected great multicultural diversity.[25]

Although one sees evidence of multiethnic churches in the book of Acts, this integration of diverse people into local churches was not without its challenges. Luke describes tensions along ethnic/linguistic lines within the Jerusalem church as Hebrew speakers and those of Hellenistic background were at odds (Acts 6:1–7), even though both groups came from Jewish backgrounds. Thankfully, the appointment of the seven quelled (at least temporarily) the pressures and the problems. Still, other integrational challenges arose later as Gentiles came to faith in Christ. When Jewish believers received news that Gentiles were responding to the gospel, many raised concerns about their full acceptance as fellow believers. Some of them were convinced that they must also be circumcised and keep the Law (Acts 15). To this point, the Jerusalem Council issued a clear statement for circulation among churches. Still, this challenge of acceptance and integration impacted the local churches in New Testament times as illustrated in books like Galatians, Romans, Ephesians, and Colossians.

What is it that constitutes a multiethnic church today? Prill defines a multiethnic church as a "church with at least two ethnically diverse groups of substantial size."[26] DeYoung gives further clarification in defining "a racially mixed congregation as one in which no one racial group is 80 percent or more of the congregation."[27] Indeed, the book of Acts describes both the struggle and the glory of integrating diverse people into multiethnic local churches. One can glean much today from these descriptions of first-century realities. Those seeking to establish multiethnic churches including migrants can expect to face challenges as the traditions, languages, cultures, expectations, and even the influences of their former faith backgrounds may seem to be at odds.

Integration into Monoethnic Churches

While the Scriptures describe multiethnic churches in the first century, they do not, however, prescribe that exclusive approach for church life today. What about churches comprised almost exclusively of a single culture?

---

25. Prill, *Global Mission on Our Doorstep*, 79–90.
26. Prill, *Global Mission on Our Doorstep*, 78.
27. DeYoung et al., *United by Faith*, 2.

That They Might Seek Him

According to Hardison, a monoethnic church "is a congregation where more than eighty percent of the church is from the same ethnicity."[28]

In many, if not most, regions of the world, the monoethnic is the norm—understandably so. The prevalence of monoethnic churches was often a reflection of the cultural reality of a specific location. Many churches throughout the world have been historically located in regions where the overwhelming majority of the people in that location were from the same cultural background, speaking the same language. Of virtual necessity and by default, then, the local church has often begun as monoethnic. As migration causes communities, cities, and regions to become more diverse, should existing monoethnic churches adapt and transition from their default setting and intentionally and strategically adjust? Or, should the fruit of ministry among migrants result in the establishment of churches specific to the language and culture of the migrants?

Whether intentional or not, Donald McGavran has played an influential role in the establishment and prioritization of monoethnic churches in missions. His "homogenous unit principle" introduced decades ago proposed that "men like to become Christians without crossing racial, linguistic, or class barriers."[29] Certainly, that principle is part of the argument for gospel contextualization described by Paul in 1 Corinthians 9.

Although this "homogenous unit principle" may reflect a desired (even preferred?) practice of contextualized evangelism, church planters have expanded that rationale to argue for the value of monoethnic over multiethnic churches. To that point, Hardison suggests four benefits of the monoethnic church:

1. Monoethnic churches help preserve culture (valued by God).
2. Monoethnic churches help Christians to retain dual identities as Christ followers and as part of their ethnic group.
3. Monoethnic churches enhance mission by enabling the church to capitalize on high level contextualization.
4. Monoethnic churches benefit from the natural connectedness of people.[30]

---

28. Hardison, "Theological Critique."
29. McGavran, *Understanding Church Growth*, 233.
30. Hardison, "Theological Critique," 154–83.

Taking Steps Toward Contextualization and Integration

There are, then, certain advantages to the monoethnic model. In seeming support of this model, Casey proposes a very pragmatic question. He writes, "I like to ask church planters, 'Is your goal to plant a multi-ethnic church or is it to reach as many as possible in this community?'"[31]

At first glance, the monoethnic approach may seem to be the most efficient, with the least number of hurdles and least need for integration. Of course, coupled with the least need for integration is potentially also the least degree of integration. One dare not be too short-sighted, however, in the selection of church models. Migrant servants and church leaders should also consider the next generations—the children and grandchildren of those migrating (as illustrated in the opening story of this chapter). This is not intended to discourage monoethnic church plants, but it is designed to encourage a prayerful, intentional, strategic plan that considers not only those responding to Christ now but also the implications for future generations. Both the mono- and multiethnic models have their place. Those planting churches among migrants need incredible wisdom in knowing how to move forward.

Integration into Mono Multiethnic Churches

More recently, Stephen Beck, a professor and church planter in Germany, has proposed and practiced another model that he calls the "mono multicultural church." According to the definition of a multiethnic church given earlier, Beck's model is still a type of multiethnic church. By design, no racial group dominates with more than 80 percent of the congregational consistency. Nevertheless, Beck differentiates this type of church and places it in a category of its own. What is it, then, that, in Beck's mind, distinguishes what he calls the "mono multicultural church" from other multiethnic approaches? He describes the "mono" aspect of the model as the church maintaining

> its identity and the defining characteristics of the basis culture ... For example, Germans love to have everything orderly, organized, and clearly defined. They believe in efficiency, thoroughness, and punctuality. Other cultures can profit from this. When migrants integrate into German society, the German church, with her basis culture, helps them to adjust to these foundational attributes of the host country.[32]

31. Wan and Casey, *Church Planting among Immigrants*, 88.
32. Beck and Bielefeldt, *Mission Mosaikkirche*, 93.

Still, according to Beck's model, place is also given for the expression of the individual cultures of the migrants. Beck continues, "In a mono/multicultural church the cultural differences in the church are respected and are integrated into church life side by side with the basis culture."[33] The basis culture will look for ways and opportunities to uphold aspects and treasures of the other cultures. In so doing, both those in the basis culture and those from other cultures are blessed.[34] Practically speaking, worship services in a mono/multicultural church give priority to the language of the basis culture. Congregants, however, have opportunity to participate in language/culture-specific small groups.

Monoethnic? Multiethnic? Mono multiethnic? Some type of theological or pragmatic argument can be made for each of these church types as they relate to migrant ministry. There is neither a biblical mandate nor a universal practical reality that points conclusively to a specific approach as the one that must be used in every situation. The model must be carefully and prayerfully chosen to best fit the specific situation in each scenario. Depending on factors such as community constituency, local church history, and ethnic compatibility, one model may be more favorable than the others. Even though Hardison points to practical advantages of a monoethnic church approach, he concludes:

> Scripture offers no injunction to be multi-ethnic or mono-ethnic. As the church labors to take the gospel across cultures, it can do so by trying to establish a multi-ethnic church or by planting or partnering with a church that is a different ethnicity. This is a matter of Christian freedom.[35]

As migration continues around the world, what was, for many, a default setting of homogenous, monoethnic churches is being challenged. Those who would seek to be fruitful must prayerfully consider the question of integrating migrants into churches that will reflect an increasing multiethnic dimension or of seeing them grow in churches that reflect their own culture of origin.

---

33. Beck and Bielefeldt, *Mission Mosaikkirche*, 94, 95.
34. Beck and Bielefeldt, *Mission Mosaikkirche*, 95–98.
35. Hardison, "Theological Critique," 152.

Taking Steps Toward Contextualization and Integration

Summary

This chapter has outlined challenging aspects of migrant integration in three overlapping arenas. In particular, dimensions of national, societal, and ecclesiological integration have been the focus. While each of these three was discussed separately, those serving in migrant ministry must recognize the vital role that each plays in the lives of migrants. Still further, they must also identify the key role that they can personally play in each of these aspects of integration. Of course, they do not own sole responsibility for migrant integration. As has been made clear, integration is a two-way street, bigger than any individual.

Integration at the national level is rooted, first of all, in the paradigm that national leaders and the nation embrace. Realism emphasizes the sovereignty of the state and a concern for its citizens. Communitarianism, meanwhile, identifies the needs of those outside of a given state sovereignty, but it sees the individual state as the one having responsibility for the first response. Cosmopolitanism underscores the needs of people and the moral responsibility of all to address those needs. In all probability, no nation purely reflects only one of those paradigms, but each nation finds itself on a continuum amongst those three.

The paradigmatic conviction of a state, then, plays a big part in immigrant integration as reflected in policy development. In particular, the paradigm will impact policies determining who, how many, and under what conditions a person might immigrate. Citizenship models (imperial, folk, republican, or multicultural) express further expectations related to migrant integration. Those who understand integration at the national level are better positioned for effective service in migrant ministry. They are in a position to come alongside of migrants in their pursuit of a visa, work permit, or citizenship and their corresponding requirements.

This chapter has also provided a summary of some of the many indicators of migrant integration in society. Means and markers provide both important stepping-stones toward and positive signs of successful integration. Connecting through bonds, bridges, and links joins migrants to other meaningful relationships and services. Five different facilitators also serve to simplify the process of integration. All of these are rooted in the two-directional rights and responsibilities of both migrants and others in their new homeland.

Societal integration is vital to the migrant's sense of well-being, as well as his/her contribution to and longevity in the destination country. As bridges, believers can connect migrants to people, services, and opportunities for things like employment and housing. They can help in areas that will contribute to the migrant's integration, like language learning, cultural adaptation, and computer skills development.

Finally, this chapter has examined the challenges of ecclesiological integration. As people from different linguistic, cultural, and faith backgrounds come to faith in Christ, integration into a local church is not simple. These lines explored the advantages and limitations of three different models for integration. The monoethnic model argues for integration of migrants into local churches that reflect the cultural/linguistic expressions of the migrant. The multiethnic model seeks to integrate people from various cultures and languages into a single local church that typically reflects the characteristics of the dominant nationality. As somewhat of a hybrid, the mono multiethnic model encourages the integration of people from various cultures while seeking to honor the unique cultural expressions of each group in the greater context of the dominant culture.

Once again, those working among migrants need great wisdom from God when it comes to local church integration. Each locality brings with it a unique blend of cultures, history, and traditions that must be considered. Prayerful care must be given to the important decision of integrating migrants into the family of God.

7

Engaging Migrants in a Digital World

Bisrat had come to appreciate the people at the Community Center. More than once, they had slowly and patiently explained to him the content of the latest official looking mailing he had received. He had attended and enjoyed the language classes offered there. The conversation café was part of his weekly routine, when other appointments did not conflict with it.

He knew that those who worked at the Community Center were Christians. In his Muslim homeland, Bisrat had been told things about Christians that had caused him to keep them at arm's length. But, over time and through his positive encounters, he discovered that those stereotypes were not entirely accurate. The truth was, he had come to appreciate those serving there. On occasion, they came to visit him. He and his wife valued the opportunity to offer them hospitality. Whenever the Community Center workers sent a text message over WhatsApp, it lifted Bisrat's spirits. Most of the relationship, however, was experienced face to face in personal encounters.

Then, in March of 2020, COVID-19 restrictions in his new homeland forced the Community Center to close. For the next several months, personal contact with workers there (and with anyone outside of his own household for that matter) was nearly impossible. Bisrat's relationships to those at the Center, once rooted in shared, in-person relationships seemed threatened.

Even though migrants may differ in their mother tongues, there is one language that many of them share in common—they speak "digital." Skills for navigating the Internet jungle help them as they transition to and establish a new life in a new land. Even if their technological awareness and abilities were limited prior to the COVID-19 pandemic, the realities of limited personal contact and freedom to accomplish the simplest of tasks have certainly encouraged them to expand their utilization of digital tools.

Thus, many migrants have a widespread familiarity with and growing need to utilize technology. For Christ followers, this reality invites the question of how they can leverage digital platforms and resources in the context of ministry among this mobile migrant population. Consequently, this chapter focuses on three areas. First of all, the basic premise of migrant use of technology will be explored. The next section focuses on the value of relationships in migrant ministry and digital methods for nurturing these relationships. Finally, the chapter outlines a sampling of digital tools that can be used specifically for disciple making.

Migrant Use of Technology

As already suggested, migrant use of technology is widespread. Alencar et al., for example, explore the topic specifically from the vantage point of refugee use of technology during their flight to their new host country. Vijayam, meanwhile, addresses this issue for migrants as an entire group from the timeframe of uprooting to integrating. He summarizes migrant use of technology into seven primary categories. This section will use Vijayam's summary as a grid for understanding some of the primary ways in which migrants use technology.

Technology Helps Migrants Facilitate Migration

At its earliest stages, media and technology often inspire the potential migrant with the idea that migration is both desirable and doable. A television broadcast may seem to point to opportunities elsewhere. Texts or social media messages from a friend or family member already in a host country seem inviting. Vijayam describes the power of these technological connections between friends and family members as they, at times, lead to chain migration. He states, "People tend to migrate to places where they have contacts, often depending on those contacts for access to the new country."[1]

Technology Helps Migrants Communicate and Connect with the Homeland

Since many migrants have left friends and family members in their country of origin, they utilize technology to stay connected with those relationally close but geographically distant. Statista estimates that there were approximately 1.67 billion registered Skype users in 2020.[2] Zoom, meanwhile, experienced an average of 300 million Zoom meetings per day at the height of the COVID pandemic. Of course, not all of these users or meetings represent migrants connecting with family members and friends. Meanwhile, WhatsApp, with its widespread availability, ease of use, and encryption technology, has become a favorite platform for migrants for texting and calling. Manjoo writes,

> for many, WhatsApp has been at the center of a newfound connectedness. Wherever there are people leaving their homes for uncharted shores, you are likely to find WhatsApp. For migrants, it has become the best way to stay connected along a route, or, once they have landed, to keep in touch with the people they left back home.[3]

Combined with other social media options such as Facebook and Instagram, migrants are able to share their lives with those not near. As Vijayam states, "These technologies give a sense of 'being present' at family occasions and being involved in each other's lives with frequent updates enabling a level of engagement that was unimaginable just a decade ago."[4]

Technology Helps Migrants Coalesce Homogenous Diaspora Communities

As migrants move from the familiar into the foreign, many of them naturally look for people who have shared their migrant journey into the

---

1. Vijayam, "Technology and Diaspora," 272.
2. Statista, "Estimated Skype User Numbers Worldwide."
3. Manjoo, "For Millions of Immigrants."
4. Vijayam, "Technology and Diaspora," 273.

unfamiliar. In many instances, they seek out those with a common cultural background. Whether they knew these people previously or not is less important. Even a stranger from their homeland can quickly become a friend in their new land. Through social media, this can happen with a selectivity and at a pace that is often not afforded through physical meetings. In the words of Vijayam:

> The Internet with all its associated technologies has made it possible for people to connect instantly from their homes and at their own pace. Social media has taken migrant networks to a new level of connectedness by creating an opportunity to build one's social capital quickly and selectively with those whom they have more in common.[5]

Meanwhile, for those fleeing the ravages of war or natural disaster, there is, at times, the need for reunification of family members and friends. Organizations have developed websites and apps to assist people in finding loved ones from whom they have been separated. REFUNITE is one of those organizations. They describe themselves as "a nonprofit tech organization whose mission is to reconnect refugee families across the globe with missing loved ones."[6]

Technology Helps Migrants by Providing a Forum for Exchange of Ideas

While there is no single location where migrant-specific ideas are exchanged, the Internet offers all kinds of information that addresses virtually any question that a migrant might ask. Vijayam points to the incredible value of search engines that make this exchange possible. Through these searches, "new immigrants seek information that is unique to their situation as newcomers, distinct from the sorts of information sought by the general population in their adopted country."[7]

---

5. Vijayam, "Technology and Diaspora," 273.
6. See https://refunite.org/about.
7. Vijayam, "Technology and Diaspora," 273.

Engaging Migrants in a Digital World

Technology Helps Migrants by Offering a Community Bulletin Board

Once again, Vijayam points to "specialized websites and web forums dedicated to educational and employment opportunities, housing, dating and even matchmaking that are targeted to specific groups of immigrants."[8] Careers4Refugees, for example, offers potential employers the space to post positions. Likewise, it allows refugees the opportunity to post their resumes. As a result, employers can look for suitable refugee candidates, and refugees can explore possible opportunities. Careers4Refugees describes itself as "a fully functioning job board which aims to assist companies interested in the refugees' cause to help them to get back on their feet."[9] Meanwhile, other digital tools such as LevelApp serve refugees in Sub-Saharan Africa as it helps them to "build a pathway out of poverty" by "extending digital work opportunities to refugees."[10]

Technology Helps Migrants to Foster Collective Action

Vijayam describes this action as two-directional. On the one hand, leaders in countries of origin use technology to invite those living in diaspora to participate in voting or to provide financial or social support. Meanwhile, migrants abroad use technology, especially social media, to garner increased awareness of and participation in issues in their homeland.[11]

Technology Helps Migrants to Facilitate Financial Transactions

Employment and economic opportunities are strong contributors to the many reasons that people choose to migrate. In addition to online banking options, many migrants utilize technology in order to send remittances to loved ones left behind in developing countries. The Global Knowledge Partnership on Migration and Development estimated the 2019 remittances to low- and middle-income countries totaled $554 million. Meanwhile, COVID realities impacted wages and employment among migrants in 2020. As a

---

8. Vijayam, "Technology and Diaspora," 274.
9. See https://careers4refugees.com.
10. See https://www.levelapp.net.
11. Vijayam, "Technology and Diaspora," 274.

result, remittances declined to an estimated $445 million.[12] While some of these remittances are made possible through person-to-person encounters in brick-and-mortar banks, many Internet-based options make it possible for migrants to transfer funds with lower fees.[13]

Beyond these technological applications among migrants in general, Alencar et al. reports how refugees use smartphones during their flight. Their research points to the smartphone as a "companion, an organizational hub, a lifeline, and a diversion."[14] As outlined earlier, the smartphone is a "companion" in that it represents connection to both home and to others in the refugee community. When used as an organizational hub, the smartphone helps to find locations, gather information, and store essential documents. It also serves as a lifeline in case of emergency or emotional discouragement. Sam George, catalyst for diasporas with the Lausanne Movement, underscores this reality by stating that "modern communication and internet technologies have come to the aid of refugees in unbelievable ways, becoming indispensable tools for finding safe passages and for sheer survival."[15] As a diversion, smartphones allow refugees to document their journey or to enjoy games, movies, and other forms of entertainment. While some refrain from such use because of things like battery life, additional cost of data packages, or limited access to Wi-Fi, others allow themselves these kinds of distractions from the stresses associated with refugee flight.

Ministry Use of Technology

As just described, many migrants make widespread use of technology for a variety of purposes. As Christian workers engage with migrants for the sake of eternity, then, they must recognize that technology offers, in many instances, familiar and frequently used tools. Additionally, recent COVID realities have moved the use of digital tools from familiar and helpful to almost necessary and essential. Because of this widespread familiarity and usage, Christian workers are wise in using digital tools in ministry among migrants.

---

12. Global Knowledge Partnership on Migration and Development, *COVID-19 Crisis Through a Migration Lens*, 4–8.
13. Vijayam, "Technology and Diaspora," 274.
14. Alencar et al., "Smartphone as a Lifeline," 835–41.
15. George, "Refugees and Technology," 127.

Engaging Migrants in a Digital World

The remainder of the chapter, then, focuses on the utilization of technology in Christian ministry among migrants. Specifically, the chapter will address two applications of technology in Christian ministry. The first is the use of technology in developing, maintaining, and nurturing relationships. The second ministry application of technology is the strategic use of digital resources for the evangelization, disciple making, and spiritual development of migrants. So, before exploring technology's use, one must recognize that it is best applied in the context of relationships.

The Value of Relationships in Migrant Ministry

From a theological standpoint, relational ministry has a sound biblical precedent as demonstrated in the life of Jesus. His very incarnation illustrated its importance years before his public ministry. The apostle John describes Jesus as a migrant himself. He was one who left his heavenly home behind to come to earth. He points out, "And the Word became flesh, and dwelt among us" (John 1:14). Thus, Christ demonstrated the priority of relationships in his ministry. Not only did he share in the reality of human existence; he also lived in close proximity to the very people he sought to influence. This importance of relationships is further depicted years later as Jesus selected his disciples. Mark's words include a clear emphasis on the relational dimension of his interaction with those he chose: "he appointed twelve, so that they would be with Him" (Mark 3:14). Later in his ministry, Christ's opponents marveled that he demonstrated such relational affinity as he dared to eat with those of reputation (Matt 9:9–13). Further, Jesus celebrated with people in life's highs by attending a wedding (John 2:1–12) and he grieved with them in life's lows by comforting good friends and raising a man from the grave after a funeral (John 11:1–46). Thus, the incarnation and ministry of Jesus model a compassionate, relational approach.

More than being modeled by the Savior, the value of relationships is further borne out in practical ministry experience in the contemporary context. Missionary statesman and former executive director of the mission agency Encompass World Partners, Tom Julien, summarizes his conviction based on decades of ministry in Europe and mission leadership. He states, "the effectiveness of any evangelistic method is in direct proportion to its personal or relational context."[16]

---

16. Julien, *Seize the Moment*, 56.

Christian workers in various countries around the world further underscore the priority of a relational context for ministry to migrants. In Germany, "Felix," a Christian worker among refugees, indicated, "Relationships are essential among most refugees coming from [the Middle East]. Everything works through relationships. One can say that nothing works outside of relationships. The culture is very much based on relationships. Things like eating, visits, meetings, and activities are all part of that." "Lily," another Christ follower and colaborer in Germany, describes relationships as "the alpha and omega." "Albert," serving in a neighboring city, describes how these essential relationships and corresponding trust "grow with every honest exchange."

In Turkey, one Christian worker points to this prioritization by saying:

> Relationships are the currency of an economy of migrant ministry. Without them, there is no movement. With healthy relationships, doors open. Maintaining connection is expected. It should be a high priority and for believers the wisdom to do this well should be something that is always covered in prayer.

Similarly, another Christian brother serving primarily among refugee immigrants in Turkey shares, "from my perspective [relationships are] essential aspects because for a refugee he already left everything behind so he allows looking for a surrogate family for him."

Workers in England report a similar priority. "Andy" writes, "We are continually challenged by the importance of a relational approach with our ministry among immigrants. This is tough for Brits who have limited time for relationship building and love to function at a conceptual level!"

Christians working among migrants in France communicate the same sentiment. "Peter" states, "Relationships are essential for effective ministry to immigrants." Serving in another region of France, "Evan" underscores the essential nature of relation while describing migrants as "hungry for relationship." He continues, "Given their context they are often either rejected (at least overlooked) or in an aid relationship. They often lack being treated like a normal human being, in a two-way relationship."

Ministry among migrants in the United States also points to the value of relationships. "Kris" describes relationships as not only critical but also as difficult work that is well worth the investment. She shares:

> Relationships are essential for meaningful ministry to immigrants. It requires effort, time, investing personal interest in them, and consistency to build trust and earn rapport. Once you know

something about their story, their culture, and their personality your gospel conversations will be personal and vibrant. It's amazing how the same gospel message has so many nuances to be able to address every life question, culture, and need. During the relationship building process, it is an opportunity to do the work of cultivating the soil of the heart by being a living testimony of God's character. I'm not suggesting a lot of time must occur before planting seeds can occur, but that those seeds that are planted and prayed for will see the most harvest if we stick around and do the work of relationship.

Clearly, the importance of relationships in ministry among migrants cannot be overstated. Christians in multiple countries and ministry contexts describe that plainly. While relationships are critical, maintaining positive relationships is not always easy. Especially in the days after their arrival, migrants in general and refugees specifically may move often. "Albert" accurately describes this as a great challenge to relationships. But the challenge is not only at the beginning. "Micah" points out that refugees often eventually move into villages without transportation and, at times, with increased demands on their time. Eventually, the refugees may even move from the area of possible reach of the church and the Christian worker.

In order to invest even more heavily in relationships and to address some of the housing needs, people like Stefan have a passion for developing creative means for providing relational bridges to refugees in Germany. Stefan leads an effort to provide apartment complexes like Hoffnungshaus (Hope House) in Leonberg, Germany. Buildings like these offer integrated living options where Christian workers live next door to refugees. In these close relationships, they are intentional about helping people with daily needs and questions while being strategic about sharing their faith. Although God is the Lord of the harvest, relational access is often a rate-limiting factor to spiritual development.

Not only does migrant mobility pose a challenge to maintaining strong relationships; so does the very fragile nature of relationships themselves. "George" describes relationships, on the one hand, as "very important." Meanwhile, he also considers them to be the "largest problem." He explains by saying, "Unfulfilled expectations and mutual injuries happen again and again." Thus, Christ followers working among migrants must understand the critical nature of relationships while also considering the corresponding challenges.

The value and challenges of relationships with migrants are clear. Churches and Christian workers desiring to impact refugees for the sake of eternity must find ways to develop and nurture relationships. They should purposefully consider how programs, events, and help offered can open doors to deepened relationships of vulnerability and trust. This will be furthered explored in chapter 8 under the topic of strategy development.

The Value of Technology in Relationships to Migrants

Not all of the nurturing of relationships happens through personal visits and face-to-face contact where communicators understand one another immediately. Here technology can play a key role. "Evan" points to the value of Google Translate where language differences prevent effective communication. This digital service now offers at least some immediate translation into one hundred languages. Depending on the language, a person can use Google Translate by typing words, saying words, or, in some instances, even taking a picture of words.[17] Although still somewhat cumbersome in comparison with fluid conversation, this technological development is light-years ahead of bilingual dictionaries that were once part of such attempts at communication.

Additionally, WhatsApp has proven to play a key role in nurturing relationships. Already in pre-COVID time, one Christian worker noted, "As I was getting started with ministry to refugees, a man gave some good advice. He said that I would need lots of time, lots of patience, lots of love, and WhatsApp." Time, patience, and love all point to the importance and necessity of this relational connection. WhatsApp, meanwhile, may seem like an unusual outlier in the list. But, in the words of Manjoo, "WhatsApp has cultivated an unusual audience: It has become the lingua franca among people who, whether by choice or by force, have left their homes for the unknown."[18] Among migrants with limited financial resources, WhatsApp provides a free means of communication provided that they have internet access. In reality, then, "time, patience, love, and WhatsApp" all indicate the value of relationship.

Although not as widely used as WhatsApp, Signal is a similar app in that it is dependent upon Internet connection, and it offers texting and calling. (Video calls are not possible with Signal.) Signal's advantage, however,

17. See https://translate.google.com/about/languages.
18. Manjoo, "For Millions of Immigrants."

is the privacy it offers.[19] At times, this added encryption that protects sensitive information such as names, locations, organizations, and spiritual references is preferred by the Christian worker or the migrant.

Even before COVID-19, then, workers had identified technological connection as an important means of nurturing relationships with migrants. Then came the pandemic. The limitations in personal contact made necessary by social distancing and stay-at-home orders did two things as it related to relational connection between Christian workers and migrants. First of all, these limitations forced Christian workers to rely more heavily than ever before on technological connection in relationships. Technology was no longer a good supplement to the preferred personal face-to-face relational encounter. It had become a primary means for relational connection and nurturing. In most ministry contexts, Christian workers made intentional, organized efforts to remain in touch with all migrants with whom workers had contact. From his German context, "Frank" shared, "We tried to do a lot through telephone. Skype, Zoom, and WhatsApp were even more important than ever." In fact, workers in the UK and in Germany both noted that this desire to express genuine concern through technological tools exposed the need for additional workers who were properly equipped.

Beyond the reality of greater dependence on technology, the restrictions caused the workers to think innovatively about the use of technology in nurturing relationships with migrants. They began to think beyond its use in a pre-COVID world in order to discover new ways of utilizing digital devices, apps, and resources to bless others relationally. Innovation is often a process of discovery. Along the way, some technological attempts proved to be only marginally helpful. "Arnold," working in Turkey, discovered, for example, that the migrants with whom they were working were not as technologically adept as suggested in the opening lines of this chapter. He described challenges related to accessibility and attention span: "It was very hard in the beginning because half of our people are not familiar with the technology, and [without] physical relationship it is hard to keep attention for long period of time."

Other innovative uses of technology were more than marginally helpful. Several learned that migrants in their circle of contacts appreciated voice messages over text messages. From her work in Turkey, "Arlene" reported, "Hearing your voice, even when you cannot be in someone's home matters. Sending a quick audio message to a family [instead of a text] to check in

---

19. See https://signal.org.

after I pray for them . . . can be powerful to continue stoking the flame of the connection even when there is distance." "Lily" pointed out how they took that idea one step further as they personalized the technological contact by sending video messages to migrants rather than just audio.

In a pre-pandemic reality, some Christian workers with appropriate language skills had physically accompanied migrants to important medical, legal, or visa related appointments. Once there, they were able to provide translation so that both the migrant and the one meeting with him/her could understand. As a result of COVID restrictions, a WhatsApp call or video conversation allowed that important translation process to take place at such critical times.

WhatsApp was also used as a means of training migrants for the use of meeting platforms such as Zoom. Consequently, help services such as language classes that were once conducted in person in a specific location moved forward. Thus, migrants were still able to continue their language learning in a relational context beyond simple, less relational apps such as Duolingo.

Other innovative uses of technology to nurture relationships and meet needs are worth noting. In Turkey, workers updated the local bank cards of some migrants to ensure that they had additional resources for caring for their financial needs and obligations. These workers also utilized apps for ordering and delivering things like food, diapers, and formula to migrants in desperate need. Also, with the increased use of technology, these attentive Christ followers recognized that migrants were exhausting their data plans more quickly. They found ways to gift data packages to migrants, for whom the financial burden was great.

In spite of the new technological options utilized in the face of restrictions in COVID realities, "Lily" summarizes her convictions well. She states, "One notices that these methods are no replacement for personal contact." While this is true, some of the technological innovation related to nurturing relationships and meeting needs in pandemic times will likely prove to be helpful over the long term and into non-pandemic conditions.

The Value of Technology in Spiritual Development

By utilizing technology, the opportunities afforded Christian workers among migrants extend beyond only those that nurture relationships. The combined realities of widespread migrant technological connection, expanding Christian digital resources, and the global Great Commission mandate have inspired Christian workers to explore technology as a tool to fruitful disciple making. Vijayam describes the widespread accessibility of these tools: "Most of the digital media tools are available at very low cost to no cost. They are available round the clock. They are available on demand. They are available almost everywhere—both in the host land and in most home lands."[20]

Even though there are a wide variety of technological tools used for disciple making outlined in this section, one must recognize each tool serves a common, unified purpose. Each finds its value in bringing people into a vital and growing relationship with Jesus Christ through the living and active Word of God (Heb 4:12). Paul described the importance of the Word of God well in Romans 10:17: "So faith *comes* from hearing, and hearing by the word of Christ." The centrality of the Word of God beyond conversion itself is further expressed by Jesus as the Great Commission includes "teaching them [disciples from the nations] to observe all that I commanded you" (Matt 28:20a). In other words, Jesus pointed to the centrality of the Word of God as he defined discipleship in terms of an obedient response to his instruction.

Peter further upheld the essential role that the Word of God plays in spiritual development as he wrote:

> for you have been born again not of seed which is perishable but imperishable, *that is*, through the living and enduring word of God. For, "All flesh is like grass, And all its glory like the flower of grass. The grass withers, And the flower falls off, But the word of the Lord endures forever." And this is the word which was preached to you.
>
> Therefore, putting aside all malice and all deceit and hypocrisy and envy and all slander, like newborn babies, long for the pure milk of the word, so that by it you may grow in respect to salvation, if you have tasted the kindness of the Lord. (1 Pet 1:23—2:3)

Reading Tools

Digital tools, then, find their value in helping migrants engage with the Scriptures in life-changing ways. While there are many different Bible apps available for general Bible reading, the YouVersion Bible app is a clear

---

20. Vijayam, "Technology and Diaspora," 270.

standout when it comes to Bible engagement. Developers describe their mission as creating "biblically centered, culturally relevant experiences that encourage and challenge people to seek God through each day."[21]

The app's prolific stats are impressive.

> Already installed on over 445 million unique devices all over the world, the Bible App offers a free Bible experience for smartphones, tablets, and online at Bible.com. Our generous partners make it possible for us to offer 2,062 Bible versions in 1,372 languages for free, and without advertising.[22]

Audio Tools

In addition to the legible Bible versions available through apps like YouVersion, other audio resources are also helpful. These find their advantage in the fact that migrants can further language skills by listening in the language of the host country. Moreover, not all people are able to read. Further still, some migrants come from oral cultures where audible communication is preferred.

Once again, YouVersion leads the way. As of late 2019, the app offered 576 audio Bibles in 421 languages.[23] Meanwhile, Bible.is is another digital tool that offers Bible reading and audio Bible text. In some instances, this resource utilizes the same audio files as YouVersion. In other instances, the developers have attempted to engage listeners with more theatrical readings of the biblical texts.[24] Finally, Story Runners, a ministry of Cru, intentionally targets those from oral cultures. Rather than reading the biblical text, they tell forty-two biblical stories. These stories are available in forty-five different languages.[25]

Video Tools

Prepared more than forty years ago, the *Jesus* film has been a classic resource for acquainting people with the life and ministry of Jesus Christ.

21. See https://www.youversion.com/mission.
22. See https://www.youversion.com/the-bible-app.
23. Shaida, "YouVersion Has 71 New Audio Bibles."
24. See http://www.bible.is.
25. See https://www.storyrunners.org.

Based primarily on the Gospel of Luke, the film traces the life and ministry of Jesus from before his birth to his ascension. Having been translated into more than 1,800 languages, the film has been viewed by an estimated six billion people. Over the years, other Christian films have been developed that can be very useful in bearing witness to Christ.[26]

The parachurch ministry Cru has adapted this project for wider use. They offer short segments of the film for viewing so that a person can select portions of the storyline of Christ's life and ministry. Additionally, Cru has developed other video resources like Magdalena and Rivka.[27]

The Bible Project offers a great variety of other widely used video resources. This ministry has developed hundreds of videos, some of which are available in roughly thirty different languages. These videos offer introductory summaries to individual books of the Bible as well as teaching on major Bible doctrines or biblical topics.[28]

The app 5fish is another audio/video resource that seeks to share the story of Jesus specifically. Offered in many languages, the app has potential application in many different contexts. It is simple in its approach and helpful to those who have little or no background in Christianity.[29]

Study Tools

While there are many different Bible study tools available through platforms like Blue Letter Bible[30] and Bible Study Tools,[31] Discovery Bible Study is another more recent development. This is a description of a Bible study method using three steps and four important questions. Thirty examples of this method are available in eleven different languages as an app for both Apple and Android Devices. These thirty examples explore Bible passages from creation to Christ. The Discovery Bible Study method itself can, however, be applied to any Bible passage.[32] The three steps of the method are as follows:

26. See https://www.jesusfilm.org/about.html.
27. See https://www.jesusfilm.org/strategies-and-tools/resources/the-app.html.
28. See https://bibleproject.com.
29. See https://5fish.mobi.
30. See https://www.blueletterbible.org.
31. See https://www.biblestudytools.com.
32. See https://discoverapp.org.

Step 1: Read the story.

Step 2: Retell the story.

Step 3: Discover the story.

The four important questions include:

1. What does the story tell me about God?
2. What does this story tell me about people (or myself)?
3. If this is really God's word for my life, how will I obey?
4. Who am I going to tell?[33]

Certainly, no attempt was made here to provide an exhaustive list. The text, audio, video, and study resources indicated above represent but the tip of a much larger iceberg of digital materials available. There are countless others that merit consideration.

Summary and Conclusions

Digital tools can serve as key resources in Christian ministry to migrants. There are many factors that contribute to the wisdom of choosing to utilize them. They are, first of all, in most cases, accessible. More and more people in even the most remote parts of the world have access to these tools through smartphones, tablets, computers, and Internet connection. Thus, these resources are virtually universally available.

The affordability of access and of the tools themselves also makes them wise choices for ministry use. Data plans, data cards, and Internet access through ethernet and wireless connections are available in many budget ranges. The free public wireless connection available in some areas also eliminate potential obstacles created by the cost of accessing the tools. In addition, the tools themselves are often free to the users.

Beyond the affordability and accessibility of these tools, migrant familiarity with the use of technology and digital resources speaks to their viability as useful tools. Among other uses, many migrants consistently use technology in their flight to their new host country, as a means of connection with loved ones in their country of origin, and as a means of accessing important information. Thus, the use of technology is not a foreign concept.

---

33. Discover App, "What Is a Discovery Bible Study?"

Engaging Migrants in a Digital World

For some Christian workers, the benefits of these tools have been obvious for more than a decade. Still, for them and for others, more recent pandemic realities have increased the utilization and accelerated the innovation of these resources. Consequently, growing numbers of Christian workers are using technology and digital resources for the purpose of the Great Commission—and they are doing so in new ways. This chapter has identified some of the most often used ways in which technology, apps, and other digital resources can be applied in enriching relationships and making disciples. Each follower of Jesus working among migrants is wise to prayerfully research the best tools for his/her ministry context.

8

Planning Your Strategy

What were the churches to do? They were part of an ethnically diverse European city. More than 22 percent of its population of 1.1 million people were born outside of the country.[1] *More specifically, they were located in a suburb of Birmingham where the immigration reporting center was situated. It was one of only fourteen centers in the whole country. Thousands of people from the nations made their way by train, bus, car, bicycle, and foot to their little corner of the city where these churches called home. Compelled by compassion for migrants and by the opportunity to bless them, they felt they had to do something. What should that be? Where could it take place? How would they go about it?*

Nine churches shared the passion. Wanting to demonstrate the unity of the body of Christ emphasized in John 17, they decided to collaborate in the hopes of strengthening their efforts and their witness. Each church brought its own denominational orientation: Anglican, Catholic, Methodist, Reformed, Quaker, and charismatic. One of the churches was located one block from the reporting center. Because of its proximity, it seemed to be the obvious location for anything they would do. Each church brought its own passions to the table.

Because of their desire to collaborate, the churches had to agree upon an approach. In the end, they decided to offer a café that would open for several hours on two days of the week. People could stop in, drink some tea,

---

1. Birmingham City Council, *2011 Census*, 12.

coffee, or juice and eat some cookies, engage in conversation, and receive free advice. In those conversations, they had opportunity to practice their English. The café was staffed by vetted volunteers from the nine churches. There were those preparing and serving the food and drink and others ready to talk. Spiritual matters were only addressed as migrants brought them up. As the migrants left, they had opportunity to pick out some food items donated by local grocery stores and bakeries to take home. In addition, the migrants could select second-hand clothing items and toys for themselves and their families.

Each church was glad for the opportunities to encourage individual migrants, even if it was only a single, isolated encounter. It was a joy for them to be Good Samaritans along the migrant's path (Luke 10:25–37). It was rewarding to think that perhaps they had served Christ by offering food, drink, and clothing to those considered by many to be "the least" (Matt 25:34–40). Still, some of them wondered if this was the most strategic thing they could do. They wondered if their efforts were moving the dial when it came to eternal impact.

IF YOU, AS THE reader, are not careful, you could possibly misread the full intention of this book. From the title, *That They Might Seek Him: An Introduction to Ministry among Migrants*, you might have expected a mere scholastic encounter with a pressing topic. Instead, the book has been designed to provide well-researched information along with practicable directives. Certainly, you as the reader will be the final judge of the degree to which this goal has been reached.

Still, in keeping with that purpose, this final chapter provides insights on how to pull the thoughts from the rest of the book together into a ministry strategy. Regardless of where you serve, the sentiment of others around you, and the people groups with whom you work, there are some guiding principles that can help you plan your approach to reaching migrants for the sake of eternity. But first, this chapter reviews some of the takeaways from each chapter.

That They Might Seek Him

Chapters 1–7 in Review

Chapter 1 outlined the magnitude of migration today. Hundreds of millions of people are living outside of their countries of origin. They have moved for a variety of reasons. Motivated by such push/pull factors as personal protection, vocational and economic opportunity, educational advancement, and family reunion, these people have chosen to live outside of their homeland. But with this widespread movement has come vast opportunities for the spread of the gospel to the nations including some of the least-reached peoples of the world.

Chapter 2 developed a theology of migration. This chapter exposed key biblical examples of migration through the grid of biblical and systematic theology by responding to the question, "How has God used migration in the Scriptures?" In the pages of the biblical record, it is clear that the Father has used migration amongst the nations as he formed them, corrected and punished them, provided for them, and as a means of making disciples of those he has redeemed.

As one serving Christ among migrants, you lack complete insight regarding God's purposes in modern-day migration. One thing is clear, however. The Father always orchestrates the time and locations of the nations with redemption in mind. As Paul stated in his address on Mars Hill:

> From one man he made all the nations, that they should inhabit the whole earth; and he marked out their appointed times in history and the boundaries of their lands. God did this so that they would seek him and perhaps reach out for him and find him, though he is not far from any one of us. (Acts 17:26–27)

You, as a Christian worker, have the privilege, then, of cooperating with God's purpose of sharing the message of Christ with those on the move and on the search for him.

Biblical examples of and overarching guidelines for ministry to migrants were the primary topics discussed in chapter 3. Rooted in their own past, empathetic, migrant experience in Egypt, the nation of Israel carried a responsibility to care for the migrants living among them. In the New Testament, God's unmistakable passion to see the nations reached resulted in the calling of Christ followers to proclaim Christ to them—whether they are a continent away or in the same county. This chapter also challenged you, as a Great Commission servant, to an approach to ministry called *prioritism*. In other words, the Scriptures invite you, in the midst of all of the

Planning Your Strategy

migrant needs, to give priority to disciple making. This does not mean that you should overlook or minimize temporal needs. These may, in reality, provide you with the very onramp for deepened relationships and gospel opportunity.

Chapter 4 introduced the terms *realism, communitarianism,* and *cosmopolitanism.* These paradigms for international relations impact policy development regarding immigration. Focusing to a greater extent on the needs of citizens and emphasizing state sovereignty, those embracing realism will tend to be more restrictive in immigration policy. At the other end of the spectrum, cosmopolitanism places a greater emphasis on global needs.

Chapter 5 sought to answer the question of the Christian's role and response to policy development. The chapter began by examining the paradigms, critiquing the frames, and analyzing the contemporary arguments that influence public opinion and policy development. In the last half of the chapter, you were equipped with practical steps—from prayer to advocacy—that you as a believer can take in the process of immigration policy development.

Ministry contextualization and migrant integration were the primary topics from chapter 6. Those serving Christ among migrants must consider the language, cultural, and religious differences. As a result of these differences, most migrants enter their new host country as excluded outsiders. But effective integration is not a responsibility they bear alone. Integration is a two-way street where both the migrant and those in the host country carry responsibilities. This chapter explored three types of integration: national, societal, and ecclesiological. You, as a representative of Jesus, are privileged to be able to come alongside the migrant pursuing citizenship, seeking inclusion in the local community, and aspiring to participate in a local body of Christ.

For many migrants, technological and digital resources are often accessible, affordable, and familiar. The application of such tools for ministry purposes was the focus of chapter 7. You can use these tools to both enrich relationships and to make disciples. As in Romans 10:8–17, the digital disciple-making resources find their value as an expression of the "good news" that you as the "preacher" can share with the "hearer." By utilizing these resources, you can expand your influence for Christ's sake beyond those times when you are able to be physically present.

Next Steps in Strategy Development

Fruitful missional ministry among migrants is a complex thing. It is not like a mathematical equation where 1 + 2 = 3. It is not like a chemical reaction in a laboratory where, when ingredients A and B are mixed in a beaker, product C always results. In other words, adding together the right mix of application from each of the preceding seven chapters does not ensure a great harvest. Like the seeds that sprout without the farmer knowing how (Mark 4:26–29), spiritual harvest is, at times, mysterious and unpredictable.

Although there is a certain mystery to migrant ministry—or any ministry for that matter—the sense of mystery does not exclude the value of strategy development. In these closing pages, then, you will be given practical thoughts designed to guide you as you seek to answer the question: "What strategy should you as an individual, as a church, or as a mission agency adopt as you engage missionally with those living outside of their country of origin?"

First of all, a biblical backdrop for and the merits of strategy development are explored. In the next portion of this chapter, a ministry model template is introduced. This template is generic enough to be applicable to any migrant mission ministry context, and yet it is specific enough to be helpful to every. Finally, this chapter closes by suggesting a metaphor of ministry essentials that should be addressed in any and every migrant ministry context.

The Biblical Background

At the risk of stating the obvious, it merits noting that all strategy development is dependent upon the plans of God. As cautioned in James 4:13–17, one dare not so carefully strategize timeframes, locations, methods, and outcomes that God's will is left out of the planning. Rather, while planning is necessary, it is subjected to the will of God. As James states, "Instead, you ought to say, 'If the Lord wills, we will live and also do this or that'" (Jas 4:15). Those engaging in mission of any kind must be reminded that "The mind of man plans his way, But the Lord directs his steps" (Prov 16:9).

Paul's second missionary journey serves as a good illustration of this reality. After Timothy joined the team, Luke reports, they were "forbidden by the Holy Spirit to speak the word in Asia" (Acts 16:6). Their next plans were also thwarted as the author continues, "and after they came to

Mysia, they were trying to go into Bithynia, and the Spirit of Jesus did not permit them" (Acts 16:7). Although the apostle had his own intentions, he subjected them, ultimately, to God's will.

Missional ministry among migrants is always dependent upon God, who is sovereign and powerful. He uses circumstances, churches, and individuals as tools for accomplishing his mission and for bringing glory to himself. While some plant and others water, the triune God is, ultimately, the one responsible for the fruit of ministry (1 Cor 3:6). All who endeavor to do anything for him should humbly and prayerfully acknowledge their dependence on him as they invite him to work. Each person who seeks to serve him must look to him for his directives. And when even the smallest of harvests is observed, he, as the Lord of the harvest (Matt 9:38), is worthy of gratitude and praise. Any kind of fruitful ministry is, in the end, the result of the movement of his gracious hand as the servant of God abides in him (John 15:1–17).

To be sure, a commitment to human methods and strategies can cause the Christian worker to be planned and regimented. In its extreme form, it relies on his/her strategic planning and neither depends upon God for his work nor looks to him for his directives. As used here, then, "strategy" development is not at all intended to imply human effort void of reliance on and directives from the Spirit of God.

Still, while recognizing dependence on and the need for directives from God, there is good reason for identifying the goals for specific migrant ministry and planning the methods for reaching those goals. In fact, there is biblical precedent for ministry strategy. Both Jesus and Paul, arguably the most prominent New Testament characters, gave evidence of having a strategy. Both of them described goals for their ministry and demonstrated methods they used for achieving them. Their ministries, then, demonstrate the merits of strategy development.

Jesus and Strategy

Christ's "strategy" is first of all evidenced in his open conversations about his ministry goals. He pointed clearly to those things he sought to accomplish. His broad stroke purpose statements are captured in passages like these:

- "the Son of Man did not come to be served, but to serve, and to give His life a ransom for many" (Matt 20:28).

- "For the Son of Man has come to seek and to save that which was lost" (Luke 19:10).

- "I came that they may have life, and have *it* abundantly" (John 10:10b).

In addition, the Savior's identity and purpose were made clear in his interaction with his disciples in Caesarea Philippi in Matthew 16. His objective is that people join Peter in recognizing him as "the Christ, the Son of the living God." (vv.13–16). And he summarized his then future (now current) plan with the words, "I will build my church" (v. 18).

Further evidence of his strategic methods for the accomplishment of these goals is also outlined in the Gospels. According to John, Christ's miracles were more than just a demonstration of his genuine compassion for people. This disciple, whom the Lord loved, indicated that the miracles of Jesus were an intentional part of his strategic methodology for people to, by faith, recognize his messiahship and become heirs of eternal life (John 20:31). Similarly, his preaching and instruction served more than his immediate listeners. His strategic instruction was also designed to serve future generations in the making of disciples, who are taught "to observe all that [Jesus] commanded" (Matt 28:20).

Robert Coleman, in his classic book *The Master Plan of Evangelism*, attempted to outline the strategy of Jesus as it related to the making and multiplying of disciples. Coleman suggested the following key terms as playing an integral part in Jesus' disciple-making strategy:

1. selection
2. association
3. consecration
4. impartation
5. demonstration
6. delegation
7. supervision
8. reproduction[2]

Thus, Jesus had clear objectives in mind as he conducted his earthly ministry. These goals caused him to be strategic in the methods he used. He leveraged these strategic methods in order to reveal himself, to enlist

2. Coleman, *Master Plan of Evangelism*.

Planning Your Strategy

the ministry of others, and to ensure that his unstoppable church would be established.

Paul and Strategy

In like manner, the apostle Paul also served God strategically with ministry objectives and corresponding methods. He described his objective in terms of his tireless efforts to "present every man complete in Christ" (Col 1:28). His methodology included taking the gospel message "to the Jew first and also to the Greek" (Rom 1:16). That statement depicted more than a theoretic prioritization. It was also expressed in his chronological approach in most cities where he ministered. Where possible, it seemed that he first sought an audience among Jews who were familiar with the Old Testament backdrop for the Messiah—often in the synagogue. Thereafter, he intentionally attempted to contact Gentiles, to whom he presented Christ. That strategic pattern is observable in the following geographic locations:

- Salamis—Acts 13:5
- Pisidian Antioch—Acts 13:14
- Iconium—Acts 14:1
- Philippi—Acts 16:13
- Thessalonica—Acts 17:1, 2
- Berea—Acts 17:10, 11
- Athens—Acts 17:16, 17
- Corinth—Acts 18:1–3
- Athens—Acts 19:1–8

Beyond this repeated methodology in the aforementioned cities, the apostle was also intentional in his selection of ministry locations. He yearned to go to Rome, the capital of the empire of the day (Acts 19:21; Rom 1:8–13). He further understood his calling to be that of taking the gospel where Christ was not yet named (Rom 15:20–21). Thus, he had his strategic sights set on Spain at the other end of the Mediterranean rim (Rom 15:22–24).

Others have attempted to describe Paul's strategy in more detail. Hesselgrave et al. have proposed one of the most widely used descriptions of the apostle's strategy in their "Pauline Cycle." In this cycle, they outline a recurring pattern observed in Paul's ministry. The important parts of this cycle include:

1. missionaries commissioned
2. audience contacted
3. gospel communicated
4. hearers converted
5. believers congregated
6. faith confirmed
7. leadership consecrated
8. believers commended
9. relationships continued
10. sending churches convened[3]

There are, then, both biblical precedents for and examples of missional strategy. Both Jesus and Paul demonstrated purpose, goals, intentionality, and methodology. Certainly, their exemplary ministry should be considered in strategy development for any migrant ministry. At the same time, one must also recognize these models (including Christ's plan for disciple making and the Pauline Cycle) for what they are—attempts to describe what key New Testament leaders have done, and not mandates that prescribe step-by-step instructions for servants today. This does not detract from their value, but it does offer latitude to Christ followers today.

A General Template

With these biblical models as a backdrop, those seeking to missionally engage migrants benefit from a template that guides in strategy development. Gailyn Van Rheenen, in his work "The Missional Helix," outlines a wise, general process for designing a more specific strategic approach in any missional context. Van Rheenen proposes that strategy development for mission ministry is best when it is rooted in theological reflection, cultural analysis, and historical perspective. He writes, "Each of these four elements

---

3. Hesselgrave et al., *Planting Churches Cross-Culturally,* 47, 48.

Planning Your Strategy

(theology, history, culture, and strategy) is essential in reflecting on and planning for all types of Christian ministry."[4]

Regarding theological reflection, Van Rheenen says, "All missiological decisions must be rooted both implicitly and explicitly in biblical theology in order to mirror the purposes and mind of God."[5] Certainly, there are many biblical priorities to consider. Among them is the development of a biblical ecclesiology wherein the nature, responsibilities, and centrality of the church come into clear focus. It is also here that workers must give biblical definition to the nature of mission. Although chapter 3 dealt with this question earlier, Christian workers must be aligned in their definition of their biblical responsibilities among migrants. Is the ministry direction vertical or horizontal? Physical or spiritual? Both? Should one be given greater priority than the other? If so, how can that priority be maintained? As part of this theological reflection, the biblical principles from Hesselgrave's Pauline Cycle and Coleman's *Master Plan of Evangelism* should also be considered.

In emphasizing the value of cultural analysis, Van Rheenen goes on to write, "intellectual colonialism results in *transplanted theologies*, reflecting the missionaries' heritage, rather than *contextualized theologies*, developed by reflecting on Scripture within the context of local languages, thought categories, and ritual patterns."[6] As has been explored in previous chapters, Christian workers among migrants have the potential challenge of multiple contextualizations simultaneously. When several people groups and cultures are represented, the work can become complicated. A worker may be dealing with an Urdu-speaking Muslim from Pakistan and a Hindi-speaking Sikh from India in the same day, or even in the same group—and all of that while serving as an American in Paris. Thus, strategy development must take these cultural realities into account. If church planting is part of the ministry, the cultural analysis will also contribute to discussions of the church model being pursued. Will it be monoethnic, multiethnic, or mono multiethnic?

Regarding historical perspective, Van Rheenen warns, "church planters must develop ministry based upon historical perspective rather than being oblivious of what has previously occurred."[7] The worker does well to

---

4. Van Rheenen, "MR #26: The Missional Helix."
5. Van Rheenen, "MR #26: The Missional Helix."
6. Van Rheenen, "MR #26: The Missional Helix."
7. Van Rheenen, "MR #26: The Missional Helix."

understand the factors that have driven the migration of those being served. Did they uproot primarily for economic reasons, educational opportunities, or in the hope of family reunion? If one, for example, is serving Syrian asylum seekers who have witnessed atrocities in their homeland and have recently traveled in a rubber boat to the Greek island of Lesvos, the ministry must recognize the historical trauma the migrants have experienced. Meanwhile, international students at Erasmus University in Rotterdam likely have a much different history that will impact the ministry methodology. The historical perspective should also include an understanding of previous missional efforts to reach migrants in that location. These kinds of questions of experiences and motivations rooted in the past must be a part of the development of ministry models.

Van Rheenen encourages, then, the formation of a strategy that grows out of the previous three elements. He invites those developing strategy to filter their approach through the question, "Does this model of praxis reflect the purposes of God within this historical, cultural context?"[8] In the end, ministry workers must be sensitive to these realities in the methods they choose.

A Practical Metaphor

No two migrant ministry situations are the same. Anyone using "The Missional Helix" approach, then, will recognize that there is no cut-and-paste, one-size-fits-all approach that can be universally applied. Still, there are more general ministry approaches that can be adapted for more specific situations. The "Four-Room Concept" is one such approach. Originally developed in a German context, "The Four-Room Concept for Fruitful Work with Muslims" is a product of the Barnabas Initiative.

The concept was birthed out of three factors:

1. German church excitement over the ministry opportunities afforded believers by the wave of asylum seekers created by the refugee crisis.

2. German church discouragement as they realized they did not know how to move beyond addressing physical needs of refugees.

---

8. Van Rheenen, "MR #26: The Missional Helix."

Planning Your Strategy

3. German believers' need for a roadmap that outlined a plan for spiritual development of refugees.[9]

While the German roots and Muslim context for the origin of the metaphor is clear, the potential application extends both beyond only Germany as the host country and Islam as the religious background of the migrants.

Before exploring this strategic metaphor, one should note that there are certain realities that the developers of the Four-Room Concept did not attempt to address. Perhaps these realities are assumed. First of all, it seems clear that the template assumes that meeting the physical needs of the migrants has great value. This aspect of ministry, in fact, seemed to be both obvious and natural. Although not specifically outlined in the template, these needs should be strategically, wisely, and appropriately addressed throughout the spiritual movement from room to room.

Secondly, the template assumes the value of spiritual development. Overall, the concept's content and the factors contributing to its creation make it clear that both the spiritual and the temporal have value. (Thus, it is useful for any who might conclude that disciple making is the only work, the most important work, or a part of the work.)

Thirdly, although a certain level of theological reflection is inherent to the template, it makes no attempt to address the historical or cultural elements that Van Rheenen recommends for strategy development. This work is still valuable and can/should be incorporated into the resultant strategy and methodology.

To be more specific about the Four-Room Concept, workers are invited to provide four different types of opportunities and interactions that move migrants along a spiritual continuum from unknown unbeliever to an integrated leader. The four rooms identify "different phases on a spiritual journey . . . different goals and gifting of those involved . . . and different tools that are available."[10]

The four rooms are:

1. Connection Room—Here, believers seek to make contact and build relationship with migrants. This could take place through serendipitous encounters or strategically planned opportunities like those made possible through intentional gathering spaces and help opportunities like an international café. It could begin with a warm hello as a Christ

---

9. Allgaier, personal cummunication with author, June 18, 2020.
10. Allgaier, personal cummunication with author, June 18, 2020.

follower shares public transportation, or it could be the result of helping a person in need of food, clothing, or language help. It is often an intentional act that glorifies God by demonstrating compassion in the form of warm engagement and/or practical help. Regardless of those things that give rise to the first encounter, the Christ follower can use that as a springboard for further encounters and for the development of a relationship. Many migrants come from polychronic cultures where relationships are valued more than time and punctuality. In these cultures, time and hospitality are of great importance. While many ministries use café-like settings as a means of meeting migrants and developing relationships, others that use programs and organizations that pair students or migrants with others as mentors, sponsors, or culture guides can open the door to connection. The Connection Room idea forces migrant workers to grapple with the question of "How do we intend to encounter and engage with migrants?"

2. Witness Room—As believers grow in relationship with refugees, they are in a better position for spiritual dialogue and sharing the message of the gospel. This dialogue can take place in the context of natural personal conversation, more formal Bible reading/study, and small group experiences.

   The best tools for use in this room are dependent upon such factors as the spiritual background of the migrant, the best language for communication, and the availability of resources. Certainly, the Christ follower's own story of personal conversion and of God's faithfulness are very meaningful. In addition, more formalized resources can be beneficial. Chapter 7 outlined many helpful digital resources. In addition, the Al Massira course is a video-based tool that many have found to be helpful. These recordings are available in more than twenty-five languages. They are designed largely for those from an Asian background. This thirteen-session course utilizes trained leaders who facilitate discussion of culturally sensitive videos that outline how the biblical prophets point to Jesus.[11] The Witness Room, then, invites the question of "How will I engage migrants with biblical truths about Jesus and his redemptive work?"

3. Discipleship Room—Those participating in the Great Commission among migrants dare not view conversion as the final goal. Although

---

11. See https://almassira.org.

Planning Your Strategy

it is certainly an important milestone in spiritual development, Jesus calls his followers to engage with "teaching them to observe all that I commanded you" (Matt 28:20). As migrants respond to the gospel by faith, believers should, then, continue to walk alongside of these new disciples. Just as the apostle Paul gave the Thessalonians the gospel and his very life, so too Christians play an important part in stimulating growth through biblical teaching and through modeling the Christian life. Some of the same resources that were effective in the Witness Room may also be useful here. The Discovery Bible Study, for example, has value at every point in Christian development. Meanwhile, *Come Follow Me* is another useful tool designed for those from Muslim backgrounds. Available in many languages, it is described as

> a discipleship course written specifically for new believers in Jesus from a Muslim background. It is relevant to the issues they face, is rooted in inductive Bible study, and for use in a regular, relational way (1:1 or in a group). It is also reproducible, so that those who complete the course can use it with others in turn.[12]

Of course, there are countless other tools that could be used as one interacts with migrants in this ministry room. The Discipleship Room invites the migrant ministry worker to consider the question, "How would God have us continue to stimulate growth among those migrants, who come to faith?"

4. Leadership Room—The church and her migrant ministry leaders should yearn to call and equip migrants to serve and lead in the local church and to share their faith with others outside of the faith. In that regard, the ministry comes full circle. The disciple being made becomes a disciple maker. It is here that Wan's description of "missions to the diaspora" becomes "missions through the diaspora" and "missions by and beyond the diaspora."[13] This intentional action requires

---

12. See https://www.come-follow-me.org.

13. Enoch Wan describes mission to the diaspora as "reaching the diaspora groups in forms of evangelism or pre-evangelistic social services, then disciple them to become worshipping communities and congregations." Further, he describes missions through the diaspora as "diaspora Christians reaching out to their kinsmen through networks of friendship and kinship in host countries, their homeland, and abroad." Finally, his concept of missions by and beyond the diaspora includes "motivating and mobilizing diaspora Christians for cross-cultural missions to other ethnic groups in their host countries, homelands, and abroad." Wan, "Introduction," 6.

character development, theological preparation, and skills training. Tools for this room include more formalized studies and resources such as the Discovery Bible Study, leadership courses, and other training tracks through organizations and institutions of higher education (especially Christian institutions).

But beyond the formalized preparation, there are also the less formal and experiential dimensions of leadership development. Hands-on service opportunities are excellent training grounds for future servant leaders. As the migrant learns by doing in the context of real ministry that could include short-term mission outreach, he/she can refine skills and further develop character while recognizing the practical implications of theological preparation. Ministry methods and tools in the Leadership Room seek to answer the question, "How will we develop servants of Jesus and leaders for His work/church?"

This general outline of the Four-Room Concept can serve as a meaningful help in strategy development. By outlining discipleship ministry phases (rooms) that are consistent with biblical teaching and common to mission ministry everywhere, its potential application is broad, including migrant ministry. By inviting the church/Christ follower to identify the appropriate methods and tools for the specific migrant ministry context, it is very versatile. As indicated earlier, one must be careful, however, to view the rooms through the lens of the specific cultural and historical context and with the felt needs of the migrant in view. Tools for each room are best identified with those realities in mind.

A Final Reassurance

If you have made the journey through this book, you have digested numbers, processed charts, learned terms, and absorbed ideas. It is possible that all of that may seem to you to be either academic or intimidating. Ministry among migrants may appear terribly challenging. Indeed, it can be. Thus, the previous chapters were, in part, designed to equip you for the complexity of effective ministry among migrants.

These final lines, however, are intended to inspire you with its simplicity. Don't miss out on the fact that God can use you, whether you can define cosmopolitanism, understand the challenges of integration, or feel comfortable with the use of technology. He uses those who love him with heart, soul, and mind. He uses those who love their neighbor as they love themselves (Matt 22:34–40).

Sally's story serves as a great example. As an American from a lazy, rural small town in Ohio, she traveled to the bustling city of Birmingham, England. As a believer, she was there to engage with migrants for six weeks. She lived in an ethnic suburb, especially utilizing a community center as her hub. The community center was short on female volunteers. Within days after her arrival, Sally was invited to lead not only a baking class but also an English conversation class. Both of those were designed to offer migrants cooking and communication skills. But they also were intentional venues for developing relationships for the sake of eternity.

Sally had no time to learn of the experiences that brought the migrants to Birmingham. She had not been trained as an ESL leader. She understood only the tip of the iceberg about cultural and faith differences represented among the participants in the two classes. In fact, she admittedly committed her own share of social and cultural faux pas given those in the room.

Still, Sally possessed patience and compassion. She saw the women through the eyes of Christ and sought to incorporate simple, natural gospel references in her conversations. The result: the women were genuinely endeared to her. In a casual and unexpected encounter with one of the women, the woman put her finger on what it was she sensed as she said of Sally, "You really do love me!"

While the words of this book were designed to equip you for the complexities of migrant ministry, may you close the back cover inspired by its simplicity. Words cited earlier from a personal interview really do merit reading again: "As I was getting started with ministry to refugees, a man gave some good advice. He said that I would need lots of time, lots of patience, lots of love, and WhatsApp."

Bibliography

Alencar, Amanda, Katerina Kondova, and Wannes Ribbens. "The Smartphone as a Lifeline: An Exploration of Refugees' Use of Mobil Communication Technologies during Their Flight." *Media, Culture & Society* 41/6 (2019) 828–44. https://journals.sagepub.com/doi/pdf/10.1177/0163443718813486.

Amstutz, Mark R. *Just Immigration: American Policy in Christian Perspective*. Grand Rapids: Eerdmans, 2017.

Bannas, Guenter von. "Flüchtlingsfrage: Merkel: 'Wir Schaffen Das.'" *Frankfurter Allgemeine Zeitung*, Politik, August 31, 2015. http://www.faz.net/1.3778484.

Bauer, Walter, and F. Wilbur Gingrich. *A Greek-English Lexicon of the New Testament and Other Early Christian Literature*. Edited by William F. Arndt and Frederick W. Danker. 2nd ed. Chicago: University of Chicago Press, 1979.

Beck, Stephen, and Frauke Bielefeldt. *Mission Mosaikkirche: Wie Gemeinden sich für Migranten und Flüchtlinge öffnen*. 2nd ed. Giessen: Brunnen, 2017.

Birmingham City Council, Planning & Growth Strategy, Planning & Regeneration. *2011 Census: Birmingham Population and Migration Topic Report*. Birmingham City Council, October 2013. 0121 303 4208. https://www.birmingham.gov.uk/download/downloads/id/9742/2011_birmingham_population_and_migration_topic_report.pdf.

Blanco, Octavio. "Immigrant Workers Are Most Likely to Have These Jobs." *CNN*, Money, March 16, 2017. https://money.cnn.com/2017/03/16/news/economy/immigrant-workers-jobs/index.html.

Blau, Francine D., Christopher D Mackie, National Academies of Sciences, Engineering, and Medicine (U.S.), Panel on the Economic and Fiscal Consequences of Immigration. *The Economic and Fiscal Consequences of Immigration*. Washington, DC: National Academies, 2016.

Bosch, David Jacobus. *Transforming Mission: Paradigm Shifts in Theology of Mission*. Maryknoll, NY: Orbis, 1991.

Brown, Oli. *Migration and Climate Change*. IOM Migration Research Series 31. Geneva: International Organization for Migration, 2008. https://www.researchgate.net/publication/253396962_Migration_and_Climate_Change.

Bundesamt für Migration und Flüchtlinge. "BAMF—Bundesamt Für Migration Und Flüchtlinge—Startseite." https://www.bamf.de/DE/Startseite/startseite_node.html.

Carroll R., M. Daniel. *The Bible and Borders: Hearing God's Word on Immigration*. Grand Rapids: Brazos, 2020.

Bibliography

———. "Diaspora and Mission in the Old Testament." In *Scattered and Gathered: A Global Compendium of Diaspora Missiology*, edited by Sadiri Joy Tiri and Tetsunao Yamamori, 100–117. Oxford: Regnum, 2016.

Casey, Anthony. "Caring for the Stranger in Our Midst: Biblical and Practical Guidelines for Ministry in the Midst of a Refugee Crisis." Presented at the Evangelical Missiological Society, Dallas, Texas, October 15, 2016.

Castelli, Francesco. "Drivers of Migration: Why Do People Move?" *Journal of Travel Medicine* 25/1 (2018) 1–7. https://doi.org/10.1093/jtm/tay040.

Coleman, Robert. *The Master Plan of Evangelism*. 2nd ed., abridged. Grand Rapids: Revell, 2010.

DeYoung, Curtiss Paul, Michael O. Emerson, George Yancey, and Karen Chai Kim. *United by Faith: The Multiracial Congregation as an Answer to the Problem of Race*. Oxford: Oxford University Press, 2003.

Discover App. "What Is a Discovery Bible Study?" https://discoverapp.org/discovery-bible-study.

"Donald Trump's Presidential Announcement Speech." *Time*, June 16, 2015. https://time.com/3923128/donald-trump-announcement-speech/.

Donnelly, Jack. *Realism and International Relations*. Cambridge: Cambridge University Press, 2000.

Elliston, Edgar J. *Introduction to Missiological Research Design*. Pasadena, CA: William Carey Library, 2011.

Enns, Paul P. *The Moody Handbook of Theology*. Rev. and expanded ed. Chicago: Moody, 2008.

Escobar, Samuel. "Migration: Avenue and Challenge to Mission." *Missiology* 31/1 (January 2003) 17–28. https://doi.org/10.1177/009182960303100104.

European Commission. "Country Responsible for Asylum Application (Dublin Regulation)." Migration and Home Affairs. https://ec.europa.eu/home-affairs/what-we-do/policies/asylum/examination-of-applicants_en.

European Union. "Working Abroad." Your Europe, Work and Retirement. https://europa.eu/youreurope/citizens/work/work-abroad/index_en.htm.

Eurostat. "Population Projections." Statistics Explained, 2015. http://ec.europa.eu/eurostat/statistics-explained/index.php/File:Five_main_citizenships_of_(non-EU)_asylum_applicants,_2016_(number_of_first_time_applicants,_rounded_figures)_YB17.png.

"Federal Benefit Eligibility for Unauthorized Immigrants." National Conference of State Legislatures, February 24, 2014. https://www.ncsl.org/research/immigration/federal-benefits-to-unauthorized-immigrants.aspx.

Flemming, Dean. *Contextualization in the New Testament: Patterns for Theology and Mission*. 3rd ed. Downers Grove, IL: InterVarsity, 2005.

George, Sam. "Refugees and Technology: Leveraging Modern Tools for Safe Passage." In *Refugee Diaspora: Missions Amid the Greatest Humanitarian Crisis of the World*, edited by Sam George and Miriam Adeney, 127–32. Littleton: William Carey, 2018.

Georges, Jayson, and Mark D. Baker. *Ministering in Honor-Shame Cultures: Biblical Foundations and Practical Essentials*. Downers Grove, IL: InterVarsity, 2016.

Gimpel, James. *Immigration Policy Opinion and the 2016 Presidential Vote: Issue Relevance in the Trump-Clinton Election*. Center for Immigration Studies, December 2017. https://cis.org/sites/default/files/2017-12/gimpel-2016-vote.pdf.

Bibliography

Global Compact for Migration. *Global Compact for Safe, Orderly, and Regular Migration. Intergovernmentally Negotiated and Agreed Outcome.* Global Compact for Migration, July 13, 2018. https://refugeesmigrants.un.org/sites/default/files/180713_agreed_outcome_global_compact_for_migration.pdf.

Global Knowledge Partnership on Migration and Development (KNOMAD), World Bank Migration and Remittances Team and Social Protection and Jobs. *COVID-19 Crisis Through a Migration Lens.* Migration and Development Brief 32. Washington, DC: World Bank Publications, April 2020. https://www.knomad.org/sites/default/files/2020-26/R8_Migration%26Remittances_brief32.pdf.

Goodman, Jack. "What's the UN Global Compact on Migration?" *BBC News*, World, December 20, 201. https://www.bbc.com/news/world-46607015.

Goodwin, Matthew, and Caitlin Milazzo. "Taking Back Control?" Investigating the Role of Immigration in the 2016 Vote for Brexit." *British Journal of Politics & International Relations* 19/3 (August 2017) 450–64. https://doi.org/10.1177%2F1369148117710799.

Grisanti, Michael. "Israel's Mission to the Nations in Isaiah 40–55: An Update." *The Master's Seminary* 9/1 (Spring 1998) 3961. https://tms.edu/msj/msj9-1-3/.

Grudem, Wayne. *Systematic Theology: An Introduction to Biblical Doctrine.* Grand Rapids: Zondervan, 2009.

Haas, Hein de, Stephen Castles, and Mark J. Miller. *The Age of Migration: International Population Movements in the Modern World.* 6th ed. New York: Guilford, 2020.

Hakimzadeh, Shirin, and D'Vera Cohn. "English Usage among Hispanics in the United States." Pew Research Center, November 29, 2007. https://www.pewresearch.org/hispanic/2007/11/29/english-usage-among-hispanics-in-the-united-states/.

Hall, Edward Twitchell. *The Silent Language.* New York: Doubleday, 1990.

Hallman, Hunter. "How Do Undocumented Immigrants Pay Federal Taxes? An Explainer." Bipartisan Policy Center, March 28, 2018. https://bipartisanpolicy.org/blog/how-do-undocumented-immigrants-pay-federal-taxes-an-explainer/.

Hardison, Richard Wilson. "A Theological Critique of the Multi-Ethnic Church Movement 2000–2013." PhD diss., Southern Baptist Theological Seminary, 2014.

Hesselgrave, David. "Redefining Holism." *Missio Nexus*, July 1, 1999. https://missionexus.org/redefining-holism/.

Hesselgrave, David F., Donald McGavran, and Jeff Reed. *Planting Churches Cross-Culturally: North America and Beyond.* 2nd ed. Grand Rapids: Baker Academic, 2000.

Houston, Tom, Robin Thomson, Ram Gidoomal, and Leiton Chinn. *The New People Next Door.* Lausanne Occasional Paper 55. Delhi: South Asian Concern for the Issue Group on Diaspora and International Students, 2005.

IDEAL Immigration. "Just How Vital Are Immigrants to the American Workforce?" April 1, 2019. https://www.idealimmigration.us/blog/how-vital-are-immigrants-to-american-workforce.

International Organization for Migration. "IOM Becomes a Related Organization to the UN." July 26, 2016. https://www.iom.int/news/iom-becomes-related-organization-un.
———. "IOM Mission." July 8, 2014. https://www.iom.int/mission.
———. *World Migration Report 2003: Managing Migration: Challenges and Responses for People on the Move.* Geneva: International Organization for Migration, 2003. https://publications.iom.int/books/world-migration-report-2003-managing-migration.

Internal Displacement Monitoring Centre. "Global Internal Displacement Database." https://www.internal-displacement.org/database/displacement-data.

Bibliography

Irregular Migration. "Irregular Migration: Stock Estimates." https://irregular-migration.net/?id=217.

Julien, Tom. *Seize the Moment: Stories of an Awesome God Empowering Ordinary People.* Winona Lake, IN: Grace Brethren International Missions, 2000.

Joshua Project. "Definitions." https://joshuaproject.net/help/definitions.

———. "Global Statistics." https://joshuaproject.net/people_groups/statistics.

———. "What Is a People Group?" https://joshuaproject.net/resources/articles/what_is_a_people_group.

Karčić, Hamza. "How Coronavirus Brought Realism Back." EURACTIV Media Network, March 23, 2020. https://www.euractiv.com/section/future-eu/opinion/how-coronavirus-brought-realism-back/.

Karzunina, Dasha. "Why Do Students Want to Study Abroad?" Quacquarelli Symonds, June 12, 2015. https://www.qs.com/why-do-students-want-to-study-abroad/.

Kenton, Will. "Organisation for Economic Co-Operation and Development (OECD)." Investopedia. https://www.investopedia.com/terms/o/oecd.asp.

King, Martin Luther, Jr. "A Knock at Midnight." Sermon, Cincinnati, Ohio, June 5, 1963. Stanford University, Martin Luther King, Jr. Research and Education Institute. https://kinginstitute.stanford.edu/king-papers/documents/knock-midnight.

Korab-Karpowicz, W. Julian. "Political Realism in International Relations." Rev. May 24, 2017. *Stanford Encyclopedia of Philosophy*, edited by Edward N. Zalta. Summer 2018 ed. https://plato.stanford.edu/archives/sum2018/entries/realism-intl-relations/.

Krogstad, Jens Manuel. "Key Facts about Refugees to the U.S." Pew Research Center, Fact Tank, October 7, 2019. https://www.pewresearch.org/fact-tank/2019/10/07/key-facts-about-refugees-to-the-u-s/.

Landgrave, Michelangelo, and Alex Nowrasteh. "Criminal Immigrants: Their Numbers, Demographics, and Countries of Origin." Immigration Research and Policy Brief 1. Washington, DC: Cato Institute, March 15, 2017. https://www.cato.org/publications/immigration-reform-bulletin/criminal-immigrants-their-numbers-demographics-countries.

Larson, Warren F. "Current Trends in Islam and Christian Mission." In *Toward Respectful Understanding and Witness among Muslims: Essays in Honor of J. Dudley Woodberry*, edited by Evelyne A. Reisacher, Joseph L. Cumming, Dean S. Gilland, and Charles E. Van Engen, 87–94. Pasadena, CA: William Carey Library, 2012.

Lausanne Diaspora Educators Consultation. "The Seoul Declaration on Diaspora Missiology." Torch Trinity Graduate School of Theology, Seoul, South Korea, November 11–14, 2009. Lausanne Movement. https://www.lausanne.org/content/statement/the-seoul-declaration-on-diaspora-missiology.

Law Offices of Charles D. Naylor. "International Waters Laws, Territories & Zones." August 30, 2019. https://naylorlaw.com/blog/international-waters-laws/.

Lazarus, Emma. *The New Colossus*. New York, 1883.

LeBor, Adam. "Angela Merkel: Europe's Conscience in the Face of a Refugee Crisis." *Newsweek*, September 5, 2015. https://www.newsweek.com/2015/09/18/angela-merkel-europe-refugee-crisis-conscience-369053.html.

Lifeway Research. *Evangelical Views on Immigration*. Lifeway Research, February 2015. http://lifewayresearch.com/wp-content/uploads/2015/03/Evangelical-Views-on-Immigration-Report.pdf.

Lingenfelter, Sherwood G., and Marvin K. Mayers. *Ministering Cross-Culturally: An Incarnational Model for Personal Relationships*. 2nd ed. Grand Rapids: Baker, 2003.

Bibliography

Little, Christopher. "The Case for Prioritism." In *Controversies in Mission*, edited by Rochelle Cathcart Scheuermann and Edward L Smither, 23–50. Pasadena, CA: William Carey Library, 2016.

Manjoo, Farhad. "For Millions of Immigrants, a Common Language: WhatsApp." *New York Times*, Technology, December 21, 2016, https://www.nytimes.com/2016/12/21/technology/for-millions-of-immigrants-a-common-language-whatsapp.html.

McGavran, Donald A. *Understanding Church Growth*. Rev. ed. Grand Rapids: Eerdmans, 1980.

McNeill, Donald P., Douglas A. Morrison, and Henri J. M. Nouwen. *Compassion: A Reflection on the Christian Life*. New York: Image/Doubleday, 2006.

"Migrants Stuck on EU Doorstep: What Is Germany Doing?" *Deutsche Welle*. https://www.dw.com/en/migrants-stuck-on-eu-doorstep-what-is-germany-doing/a-52615791.

Migration Data Portal. "Family Migration." https://migrationdataportal.org/themes/family-migration.

Murphy, Francois. "Austria to Shun Global Migration Pact, Fearing Creep in Human Rights." Reuters, October 31, 2018. https://www.reuters.com/article/us-un-migrants-austria-idUSKCN1N50JZ.

National Park Service. "Abolition." https://www.nps.gov/stli/learn/historyculture/abolition.htm.

———. "The Immigrant's Statue—Statue of Liberty National Monument." https://www.nps.gov/stli/learn/historyculture/the-immigrants-statue.htm.

Ndofor-Tah, Carolyn, Alison Strang, Jenny Phillimore, Linda Morrice, Lucy Michael, Patrick Wood, and Jon Simmons. *Home Office Indicators of Integration Framework 2019*. 3rd ed. Home Office Research Report 109. London: United Kingdom Home Office, 2019. Accessed October 25, 2020. https://assets.publishing.service.gov.uk/government/uploads/system/uploads/attachment_data/file/835573/home-office-indicators-of-integration-framework-2019-horr109.pdf.

Nehrbass, Kenneth. *God's Image and Global Cultures: Integrating Faith and Culture in the Twenty-First Century*. Eugene, OR: Cascade, 2016.

"Nepal Earthquake: What Happened and How Is the Country Rebuilding?" *BBC*, Newsround, April 25, 2016. Accessed January 22, 2020. https://www.bbc.co.uk/newsround/36129992.

Newport, Frank. "In U.S., Support for Decreasing Immigration Holds Steady." Gallup, August 24, 2016. https://news.gallup.com/poll/194819/support-decreasing-immigration-holds-steady.aspx.

Nowrasteh, Alex. "Terrorists by Immigration Status and Nationality: A Risk Analysis, 1975–2017." Policy Analysis No. 866. Washington, DC: Cato Institute, May 7, 2019. https://www.cato.org/publications/policy-analysis/terrorists-immigration-status-nationality-risk-analysis-1975-2017.

Ökumenische Bundesarbeitsgemeinschaft, Asyl in Der Kirche. „Welcome: German Ecumenical Committee on Church Asylum." https://www.kirchenasyl.de/herzlich-willkommen/welcome/.

Organisation for Economic Co-operation and Development. *International Migration Outlook 2019*. Paris: OECD, 2019. https://doi.org/10.1787/c3e35eec-en.

Orosco, Jose-Antonio. *Toppling the Melting Pot: Immigration and Multiculturalism in American Pragmatism*. Bloomington, IN: Indiana University Press, 2016.

Bibliography

Ott, Craig, Stephen J. Strauss, and Timothy C. Tennent. *Encountering Theology of Mission: Biblical Foundations, Historical Developments, and Contemporary Issues*. Grand Rapids: Baker Academic, 2010.
Padilla, C René. "Holistic Mission." In *Holistic Mission*, edited by Evvy Hay Campbell, 11–23. Lausanne Occasional Paper 33. Produced by the Issue Group on Holistic Mission for the 2004 Forum for World Evangelization, Pattaya, Thailand, September 29–October 5, 2004. Lausanne Committee for World Evangelization, 2005. https://www.lausanne.org/wp-content/uploads/2007/06/LOP33_IG4.pdf.
Paris, Francesca. "Protesters and Police Clash in Brussels at Rally Against UN Migration Pact." *NPR*, December 17, 2018. https://www.npr.org/2018/12/17/677295414/protesters-clash-with-police-in-brussels-at-rally-against-un-migration-pact.
"Passenger Numbers to Hit 8.2bn by 2037—IATA Report." *Airlines.*, November 26, 2018. https://www.airlines.iata.org/news/passenger-numbers-to-hit-82bn-by-2037-iata-report.
Payne, J. D. *Strangers Next Door: Immigration, Migration and Mission*. Downers Grove, IL: InterVarsity, 2012.
Piper, John. *Let the Nations Be Glad!: The Supremacy of God in Missions*. 3rd ed. Grand Rapids: Baker Academic, 2010.
Prill, Thorsten. *Global Mission on Our Doorstep: Forced Migration and the Future of the Church*. N.p.: GRIN, 2017.
Remigio, Amador, Jr. "Globalization, Diasporas, Urbanization and Pluralism in the 21st Century: A Compelling Narrative for the Missio Dei?" In *Scattered and Gathered: A Global Compendium of Diaspora Missiology*, edited by Sadiri Joy Tiri and Tetsunao Yamamori, 10–48. Oxford: Regnum, 2016.
Rosen, Eric. "Over 4 Billion Passengers Flew in 2017 Setting New Travel Record." *Forbes* September 8, 2018. https://www.forbes.com/sites/ericrosen/2018/09/08/over-4-billion-passengers-flew-in-2017-setting-new-travel-record/.
Ryrie, Charles Caldwell. *Biblical Theology of the New Testament*. Chicago: Moody, 1959.
Santos, Narry F. "Exploring the Major Dispersion Terms and Realities in the Bible." In *Diaspora Missiology: Theory, Methodology, and Practice*, edited by Enoch Wan, 35–52. 2nd ed. Portland, OR: Institute of Diaspora Studies of USA, Western Seminary, 2014.
"Seehofer distanziert sich von Merkels 'Wir schaffen das.'" *Die Presse*, July 30, 2016. https://diepresse.com/home/politik/aussenpolitik/5060273/Seehofer-distanziert-sich-von-Merkels-Wir-schaffen-das.
Shadle, Matthew Allen. "Interrogating the Legal/Illegal Frame: Trump Administration Immigration Policy and the Christian Response." *Journal of Ecumenical Studies* 55/1 (2020) 91–103. https://ixtheo.de/Record/1725841487.
Shaida, John. "YouVersion Has 71 New Audio Bibles, in 68 Languages." Life.Church/YouVersion, October 30, 2019. https://blog.youversion.com/2019/10/new-audio-bibles-and-languages-q3-youversion-bible-app/.
Sironi, Alice, Celine Bauloz, and Miliene Emmanuel, eds. *Glossary on Migration*. International Migration Law 34. Geneva: International Organization for Migration, 2019. https://publications.iom.int/system/files/pdf/iml_34_glossary.pdf.
Soerens, Matthew, and Jenny Yang. *Welcoming the Stranger: Justice, Compassion & Truth in the Immigration Debate*. Downers Grove, IL: InterVarsity, 2018.
Spitters, Denny, and Matthew Ellison. *When Everything Is Mission*. N.p.: Pioneers USA and Sixteen:Fifteen, 2017.

Bibliography

Statista. "Estimated Skype User Numbers Worldwide from 2009 to 2024." https://www.statista.com/statistics/820384/estimated-number-skype-users-worldwide/.

———. "Length of the World's Railway Network in 2015 and 2020." https://www.statista.com/statistics/619184/metro-networks-worldwide-track-distribution/.

———. "Number of Vehicles in Use Worldwide from 2006 to 2015." https://www.statista.com/statistics/281134/number-of-vehicles-in-use-worldwide/.

Stenschke, Christoph. "Migration and Mission According to the Book of Acts." *Missionalia* 44/2 (December 2016) 129–51. http://www.scielo.org.za/pdf/mission/v44n2/03.pdf.

Storti, Craig. *Figuring Foreigners Out: A Practical Guide*. Boston: Intercultural, 1999.

Tennent, Timothy. *Invitation to World Missions: A Trinitarian Missiology for the Twenty-First Century*. 2nd ed. Grand Rapids: Kregel, 2010.

Tira, Sadiri Joy. "Preface." In *Scattered and Gathered: A Global Compendium of Diaspora Missiology*, edited by Sadiri Joy Tiri and Tetsunao Yamamori, xv–xxii. Oxford: Regnum, 2016.

"Travel Channel." *Huffpost*. https://www.huffpost.com/author/travel-channel.

UK Home Office. "About Us." https://www.gov.uk/government/organisations/home-office/about.

UN. "International Migrants Day: Background." https://www.un.org/en/observances/migrants-day/background.

———. "What We Do." https://www.un.org/en/sections/what-we-do/.

UN Department of Economic and Social Affairs. *International Migration Policies: Government Views and Priorities*. ST/ESA/SER.A/342. New York: United Nations, 2013. https://www.un.org/en/development/desa/population/publications/pdf/policy/InternationalMigrationPolicies2013/Report%20PDFs/z_International%20Migration%20Policies%20Full%20Report.pdf.

———. "International Migrant Stock: The 2017 Revision." 2017. https://www.un.org/en/development/desa/population/migration/data/estimates2/estimates17.asp.

———. "International Migrant Stock 2019." https://www.un.org/en/development/desa/population/migration/data/estimates2/estimates19.asp.

———. *International Migration Report 2017: Highlights*. ST/ESA/SER.A/404. New York: United Nations, 2017. https://www.un.org/en/development/desa/population/migration/publications/migrationreport/docs/MigrationReport2017_Highlights.pdf.

———. *Recommendations on Statistics of International Migration*. Revision 1. ST/ESA/SER.M/58/Rev.1. New York: United Nations, 1998. https://unstats.un.org/unsd/publication/seriesm/seriesm_58rev1e.pdf.

UN High Commissioner for Refugees. *Global Trends: Forced Displacement in 2018*. Geneva: United Nations High Commission on Refugees, June 18, 2019. https://reliefweb.int/sites/reliefweb.int/files/resources/5d08d7ee7_0.pdf.

———. "History of UNHCR." https://www.unhcr.org/history-of-unhcr.html.

UNESCO Institute for Statistics. "Education: Outbound Internationally Mobile Students by Host Region." http://data.uis.unesco.org/Index.aspx?queryid=172.

US Census Bureau. "U.S. Census Bureau Current Population." https://www.census.gov/popclock/print.php?component=counter.

US Citizenship and Immigration Services. "Asylum." August 25, 2020. https://www.uscis.gov/humanitarian/refugees-and-asylum/asylum.

———. "Citizenship and Naturalization." July 5, 2020. https://www.uscis.gov/citizenship/learn-about-citizenship/citizenship-and-naturalization.

Bibliography

———. "Green Card Through the Diversity Immigrant Visa Program." January 11, 2018. https://www.uscis.gov/green-card/green-card-eligibility/green-card-through-the-diversity-immigrant-visa-program.

———. "Refugees." May 7, 2020. https://www.uscis.gov/humanitarian/refugees-and-asylum/refugees.

US Department of Homeland Security. "Lawful Permanent Residents (LPR)." April 4, 2016. https://www.dhs.gov/immigration-statistics/lawful-permanent-residents.

US Department of State, Bureau of Population, Refugees, and Migration. "About Refugee Admissions." https://www.state.gov/refugee-admissions/about/.

Van Praag, Oriana. "Understanding the Venezuelan Refugee Crisis." Wilson Center, September 13, 2019. https://www.wilsoncenter.org/article/understanding-the-venezuelan-refugee-crisis.

Van Rheenen, Gailyn. "MR #26: The Missional Helix: Example of Church Planting." *Missional Reflections* (blog), January 20, 2011. http://missiology.com/blog/GVR-MR-26-The-Missional-Helix-Example-of-Church-Planting.

Van Til, Henry R. *The Calvinistic Concept of Culture*. Grand Rapids: Baker Academic, 2001.

Vidal, Elisa, and Jasper Tjaden. *Global Migration Indicators 2018*. Berlin: International Organization for Migration, Global Migration Data Analysis Centre. https://publications.iom.int/system/files/pdf/global_migration_indicators_2018.pdf.

Vijayam, Joseph. "Technology and Diaspora." In *Scattered and Gathered: A Global Compendium of Diaspora Missiology*, edited by Sadiri Joy Tiri and Tetsunao Yamamori, 269–77. Oxford: Regnum, 2016.

Walzer, Michael. *Spheres of Justice: A Defense of Pluralism and Equality*. New York: Basic, 1983.

Wan, Enoch. "Diachronic Overview of Christian Missions to Diaspora Groups." In *Diaspora Missiology: Theory, Methodology, and Practice*, edited by Enoch Wan, 161–74. 2nd ed. Portland, OR: Institute of Diaspora Studies of USA, Western Seminary, 2014.

———, ed. "Introduction." In *Diaspora Missiology: Theory, Methodology, and Practice*, edited by Enoch Wan, 3–9. 2nd ed. Portland, OR: Institute of Diaspora Studies of USA, Western Seminary, 2014.

Wan, Enoch, and Anthony Casey. *Church Planting among Immigrants in US Urban Centers: The Where, Why, and How of Diaspora*. CreateSpace Independent Publishing Platform, 2016.

Wickramasinghe, A. A. I. N., and Wimitapure Wimalaratana. "International Migration and Migration Theories." *Social Affairs: A Journal for the Social Sciences* 1/5 (Fall 2016) 13–32.

World Population Review. "Bangladesh Population 2020." http://worldpopulationreview.com/countries/bangladesh-population/.

———. "Namibia Population 2020." http://worldpopulationreview.com/countries/namibia-population/.

Worldometer. "World Demographics (2020)." https://www.worldometers.info/demographics/world-demographics/#broad-age.

Wright, Christopher. "Holistic Mission." Presented at the Wycliffe Global Alliance, May 11, 2012. http://www.wycliffe.net/missiology?id=2723.

———. "A Sacred Human Condition: An Old Testament Refugee Perspective." In *Refugee Diaspora: Missions Amid the Greatest Humanitarian Crisis of the World*, edited by Sam George and Miriam Adeney, 143–52. Pasadena, CA: William Carey, 2018.

Bibliography

Wright, Steph. "The World's Most Densely Populated Cities." WorldAtlas, October 4, 2020. https://www.worldatlas.com/articles/the-world-s-most-densely-populated-cities.html.

Zangwill, Israel. *The Melting Pot*. 1908. New York: American Jewish Book, 1921. Project Gutenberg, December 18, 2007. https://www.gutenberg.org/files/23893/23893-h/23893-h.htm.

Zehnder, Markus. "The Bible and Immigration" (podcast). *Think Biblically*, June 14, 2018. Biola University. https://www.biola.edu/blogs/think-biblically/2018/the-bible-and-immigration.

www.ingramcontent.com/pod-product-compliance
Lightning Source LLC
Chambersburg PA
CBHW051936160426
43198CB00013B/2175